THE
MINDFUL
FAMILY
GUIDEBOOK

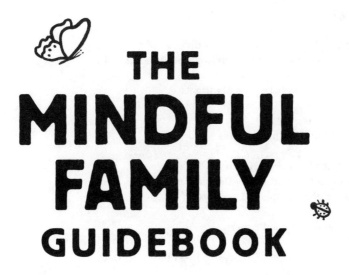

THE
MINDFUL
FAMILY
GUIDEBOOK

RECONNECT WITH SPIRIT, NATURE, AND THE PEOPLE YOU LOVE

✦ ✦ ✦

RENDA DIONNE MADRIGAL

**PARALLAX
PRESS**

PARALLAX.ORG

Parallax Press
2236B Sixth Street
Berkeley, CA 94707
parallax.org

Parallax Press is the publishing division of
Plum Village Community of Engaged Buddhism, Inc.

Cover art by Amelia Heron
Cover and text design by Debbie Berne
Author photograph by Lori Brystan

Printed on recycled paper

Library of Congress Cataloging-in-Publication Data

Names: Madrigal, Renda Dionne, author.
Title: The mindful family guidebook : reconnect with spirit, nature, and the
    people you love / Renda Dionne Madrigal.
Description: Berkeley, California : Parallax Press, 2021. | Includes
    bibliographical references.
Identifiers: LCCN 2021004830 (print) | LCCN 2021004831 (ebook) |
    ISBN 9781946764782 (trade paperback) | ISBN 9781946764799 (ebook)
Subjects: LCSH: Families—Psychological aspects. | Mindfulness (Psychology)
    | Manners and customs—Psychological aspects.
Classification: LCC HQ519 .M33 2021 (print) | LCC HQ519 (ebook) |
    DDC 306.85—dc23
LC record available at https://lccn.loc.gov/2021004830
LC ebook record available at https://lccn.loc.gov/2021004831

1 2 3 4 5 / 25 24 23 22 21

For Luke, who made everything possible
And the girls, Isabella and Sophia, my purpose
And my mom and dad, who believed
And, of course, the ancestors . . .

CONTENTS

BEGINNINGS: INITIATION

*Once you make a decision, the universe
conspires to make it happen.*

—Ralph Waldo Emerson

So here you are—you picked up the book. Something, an instinct perhaps, led you here. Where will this journey lead? Well, that really depends on you. Let's start with a proper greeting. In a proper welcoming we would be face to face, but since this is a book, I'll have to welcome you with words that are carried on the wind, blown into the pages of what was a tree or into some mysterious electronic font. Welcome to the journey . . . your journey.

I have a confession to make. I want to direct your awareness to a more instinctual, ancient orientation. One that has deep roots to sustain not only your family, but all of humanity. A long time ago, what we now call "mindfulness" was practiced by people all over the world. It is an ancient way of being aware and present to life as it is. In one of the oldest translations of Buddhist texts, the Sanskrit word *smrti* or "mindfulness" means "to remember"; the teachings of the Buddha and his students codified methods of practicing mindfulness that are still followed today. In many ways, this book is about remembering things that have sustained our ancestors and our entire human family for most of the time that we have existed on the planet. Things that we have mostly forgotten in the industrial and technological ages of the last two centuries. Things that matter for our health and happiness as well as for our planet.

This book draws on the knowledge of my heritage, my family, and the teachings I've received, and, in my turn, given to others. I am a member of the Turtle Mountain Band of Chippewa Indians, the wife of a Cahuilla traditions keeper, and a mother of two girls. I am also a certified mindfulness facilitator and a mentor with the Mindfulness Awareness Research Center (MARC) Teacher Training Program at the University of California, Los Angeles. In my day job, I serve my community as a clinical psychologist.

I started learning about mindfulness in the 1990s when I was in my twenties and in graduate school. A sage therapist told me that if I wanted to ease my own suffering, I should attend a meditation retreat by Vietnamese Zen Buddhist master Thich Nhat Hanh, who was visiting the campus of the University of California, Santa Barbara. I had never heard of him, nor had I attended a retreat before, but I wanted to learn and was willing to try. I was deeply impressed by the wisdom of this humble monk and the gentle happiness of the people around him. This first encounter with mindfulness would lead me to explore the practices in this Buddhist tradition, which gave me a sense of calm joy.

Jumping forward to 2011, I had lost touch with my mindfulness practice, and I was disillusioned with what was happening in my life and in the world. It started with my work life, which had come to feel like a series of stressors and was no longer fulfilling. Then my husband had a heart attack and underwent open-heart surgery. Our finances were drying up and our future looked gloomy and insecure. I didn't know how we would pay our bills. I was overcome with anxiety and dread, and worried that I couldn't be a good mother for my children and that my family would completely unravel. I sank into a deep depression, and somewhere in the midst of this period, a voice came through to wake me up.

I was in my living room. My husband had left the television on to his favorite show at the time—*Book TV*. Pulitzer Prize–winning journalist Chris Hedges was talking about the percentage of the world population living on less than two dollars a day.

I noticed two things. One: There was a tenderness I felt in my chest when I paid attention with an open heart. It made my own struggles more bearable, not because my suffering was less than theirs, but because I understood the interconnected nature of our suffering; I could be them, and they could be me, but for our circumstances. I could see the causes of our suffering more clearly. The second thing I noticed as was that I was becoming angrier at society as I continued to bear witness to the atrocities going on in the world. Of course, I had heard statements like this about poverty before, but until that day I had never been emotionally impacted. I really heard the words, understood the suffering that lay behind them.

As an American Indian, it's easy to be angry when you know your own history. When you understand that over 90 percent of the Indigenous population on this continent died as a result of European colonization; that the people remaining are suffering horrible health outcomes, and that Indigenous communities all over the world live with similar conditions, it is only natural to feel rage and despair.

In my life and practice, I started to see the impact of colonization on people all around me. This clarity both enraged and empowered me. I became worried that my heart would harden and turn black, and about the effect of this negativity on my marriage and my daughters. I couldn't ignore it anymore, but I didn't want to be filled with hate. How could I look at the negativity that exists in the world and not become engulfed in it too? My instincts were telling me that to deal with what was happening in my own life and in the world, I would need to immerse myself in mindfulness practice, and somehow, bring it to my family. That's when I started wondering how Thich Nhat Hanh was doing.

I knew he lived in France, that he was getting older, and I wondered how much longer he would be actively teaching in the world. I Googled him, and was astonished to learn how accessible mindfulness had become in the United States. When I say accessible, I mean that in the nineties no one was talking about mindfulness for the most part, but in 2011 it was popping up in prestigious Western institutions like the University of California, Stanford, and Oxford University in England. I signed up for a yearlong mindfulness facilitation program at the University of California, Los Angeles (UCLA), then mindfulness programs for teaching families and young people. I set an intention to incorporate mindfulness teaching into everything I did. Year after year, I led groups on Mindfulness for Indigenous Decolonization, a supplement for substance abuse and domestic violence treatment, Mindful Parenting, Mindful Families, Mindful Storytelling, Mindfulness for Social Workers and started a center—Mindful Practice Incorporated. But, most importantly, I started and maintained a personal practice of mindfulness on a daily basis.

Mindfulness has helped me through the most difficult times of my life and it has brought protection, health, well-being, and connection to my family. Now, exactly twenty years on from my first encounter with the practice, I can say that it is the greatest gift, along with the strength of their ancestral heritage, that I have given my children.

So, what *is* this precious gift of mindfulness? In addition to a way of being present, mindfulness is a practice involving attention and attitude. Our attention is one of the most powerful tools available to us as human beings, but in our modern education system, we aren't taught how to acknowledge and strengthen it. Mindfulness practices guide us in training our attention to be present to what's happening now and not distracted by and lost in all the things happening around us. The attitude that we cultivate with this practice is one of curiosity and kindness. With this focus, we gain insight that helps us respectfully connect to ourselves, each other, and the larger world in a way that improves our concentration and performance; benefits our health; leaves us feeling happier and more at peace; and leads to better choices.

How does mindfulness help, practically speaking? One day I picked my ten-year-old daughter up from school for a doctor's appointment where she was going to get a shot. Getting injections is terrifying for most elementary school children, and few kids go willingly to get what my husband calls "the big fat needle." Sitting in the back seat of our car on the way to the doctor's office, my daughter practiced mindful breathing for a few minutes, then said, "Mindfulness does help. It helps me realize that a shot is not so bad . . . if you compare it to the dentist."

Once I gave a talk for a class of school counselors at San Diego State University, on a day that my oldest daughter (fourteen at the time) was out of school, so she tagged along. Toward the end of the talk, I asked her to answer one of the student's questions about how mindfulness helps her. She said something I'll always remember: "It helps you be more aware, and that awareness helps with everything." The greater awareness that comes with mindfulness practice helps us to remember who we really are. And, when we remember who we really are, we can better align ourselves with what matters most, and when we do that, the universe steps up to meet us.

When I started practicing mindfulness, I wanted to share it with my family, but it was hard then to find mindfulness classes for children and impossible to find places where families could practice together on a regular basis. Since I couldn't find anything where I lived, I started practicing mindfulness with families I was working with in a tribal community. This led to Mindful Family Workshops, and that's how this book came about.

The Mindful Family Guidebook is a journey about protection, connection, and nourishment for all ages with the people who are most important to you: your family. It is an experiential journey guided by traditional wisdom, science, and direct experience. The practices in this book reawaken ancient intuitive awareness as a guide for the journey forward and help you to intentionally cultivate your connection to your ancestors, each other, and the larger world. When families are mindful together, they stay connected through the stages of their children's lives from preschool through the teen years into adulthood. Families who feel connected to one another have a greater sense of well-being. It doesn't require an academic study to know that such families are healthier and happier.

The first six chapters of this book build a foundation of mindfulness and promote respectful family connection. Topics include family visioning, connecting to roots, family circles, family joy, family mealtimes, and family rhythms. Chapters seven through ten focus on maintaining connection and respect while handling family challenges and distractions and linking your family to your larger community. Topics include: family peacemaking, family community connection, and family protection.

There are eight stages to complete on the mindful family journey. This book is laid out in such a way that you can take the journey over the course of a year, but you can also dive in at any point and choose a chapter to follow. Most chapters are meant to be done over a month, with the exception of chapters 2 and 7, which each take longer; I recommend two months each.

For this book, you will need to reconnect with your instincts, your ancestors, and with what matters most—your family. Information is presented in the form of guided mindfulness meditation, storytelling, improvisational instinct-based games, and nature connections. The practices and home activities are listed in a resources section at the end of each chapter, and there is also a Mindful Families website that has audio links to the recommended mindfulness practices.

To benefit from all the activities in this book, you will need a journal to write in and a folder to keep any loose sheets. Set aside time for yourself to do the initial activities and reflections to prepare to implement family-based activities. If you don't already have a regular mindfulness practice, I recommend that you do your own foundational practice, the five-minute North Star Breathing exercise from chapter 1, on a daily basis for five days before introducing it to your family. Beginning the practice first will nourish you, and give you energy so that you can hold the circle as you bring your family along on this path.

So, going back to the original question at the start of this book, where will this journey lead? It is my deepest intention with this book to help you find your way back to the natural ways of your ancestors, to help you remember things that give you deep roots to protect, sustain, and spiritually nourish yourself and your family.

...

Congratulations. You have started your journey. Now, find a journal to write in and a notebook to keep your family stories. Gather paper and simple art supplies for yourself and your children, appropriate for their age. Find time in your family calendar for everyone to be on the path of mindfulness together—just an hour once a week to begin can set you on your way. You will progress at the pace that is right for your family. Set aside time in your days for self-reflection and journaling to nourish yourself and give yourself energy and inspiration.

CHAPTER 1

FAMILY VISIONING

Your soul knows the geography of your destiny. Your soul alone has the map of your future, therefore you can trust this indirect, oblique side of yourself. If you do, it will take you where you need to go, but more important it will teach you a kindness of rhythm in your journey.

—John O'Donohue

Learning to Breathe

I had lost my direction. I was rolling full steam ahead on the "railway to progress" set forth for me centuries ago by societal forces that told me what comprises a good life. *Work hard and make money, so you can be worthy.* As an American Indian with a doctorate, I was 1 percent of the other 1 percent, an academic success story. I had figured out my place in this modern society and was on my way. *This was progress,* I thought, except whenever I stopped for a moment, I couldn't help but notice feeling like a crushing boulder was sitting on top of me, whispering, "Something is wrong." Mostly, I ignored it and pushed through my forties.

On the way to school one morning, I yelled at my then five-year-old daughter who was just learning to read to keep doing her flashcards. It didn't matter how it got done, just that it got done. I would apologize later. Right now, I had to get her to school and get back to my important work. Deep down, I knew that my life was out of balance, but I didn't have time to stop. I didn't have time to question what the boulder was that was weighing me down, causing the bad feeling in my stomach; and if I kept moving fast enough, or was distracted enough, I barely noticed it. Even if I had figured out that the boulder was a mass of my suppressed instincts and intuition, I wouldn't have known what to do with that instinctual wisdom, especially if it pushed me up against modern society's story of what a "good life" is supposed to look like. According to dictionaries, intuition is the ability "to understand something immediately, without the need for conscious reasoning." I knew that such knowledge that comes from our instincts is frequently ignored or even frowned upon in today's world, where good decision-making is based on data viewed through a socially constructed lens that defines what is good and bad. Intuition is not limited by social constructs of who we are supposed to be. Intuition lets us access a knowing that is within us. Modern society prefers things to be tamer and more controlled, more like a zoo than the Amazon rainforest.

What do we know about animals that live in zoos? In the zoo, animals exhibit abnormal behavior. They have a difficult time breeding; their lifespans are shorter, and they develop repetitive, obsessive behaviors like pacing and picking their skin to the point of self-mutilation. I thought tigers in zoos paced for exercise, but apparently, it's due to stress. Tigers in zoos pace 48 percent of the time, but in the natural environment, they spend most of their time—twenty hours a day—resting.

Animals are healthier in natural environments than they are in artificial ones like zoos, and so are we. How many of our psychological behaviors and habits are our human version of the tiger's pacing in confinement? Mindfulness practice helps us stop pacing and start listening to ourselves. How often do we really pay attention to what we need instinctually, even down to the pacing of our day? Do we feel that need we have for space in order to integrate our learning and experiences, to connect with ourselves and our families in the way that we want to, or do we just yell to get our kids out the door day after day, because that's the cage we are in? When I began paying attention to my instincts, I realized that leading "the good life" was leading me to a kind of psychological and spiritual malnourishment.

To save myself and my family, I had to recalibrate. I had to slow down and reorient myself away from artificial, external markers to a more internal and instinctual source of guidance. Something rooted deep inside myself, a wisdom that had sustained my ancestors, a strength that is also in my DNA. To listen to my own instincts, I first had to learn to stop and notice.

Stopping may seem a simple action, yet it is revolutionary in its effect. In our family lives, going to bed earlier, or not scheduling both days of a weekend, or letting go of some commitments are small steps that are surprisingly powerful. On the societal level, we've seen how the great pause in our industrious economic activities caused by the 2020 COVID-19 pandemic has had far-reaching consequences on almost every aspect of our world. In our always-rushing, overscheduled daily lives, stopping what we are doing can be a challenge, and it can even feel uncomfortable because we're not used to our natural state of stillness any more. One of the best ways I know how to enjoy being still is by learning to breathe with full awareness.

North Star Breathing: A Formal Stopping and Noticing Practice

North Star Breathing is a formal learning-to-breathe practice. It builds the skills of stopping and noticing what is happening in the present, and it helps us orient our attention to our bodies and minds in the here and now. The breath is a good anchor for this practice because it is always available to us in the present moment; it just takes a shift in our attention to remember this vital connection to life that is happening whether we are aware of it or not. Like the North Star, its existence has the quality of stillness, even when everything else is moving around it.

To prepare for North Star Breathing, find a place where you won't be distracted. Plan to practice for about five minutes. You can read the directions and do the practice yourself or you can listen to a guided North Star Breathing on the Mindful Practice website.

NORTH STAR BREATHING

Sit in an upright but comfortable position. With eyes softly closed, bring to mind a bright star sitting still in the sky. That's the North Star. Imagine breathing in from the North Star and breathing out to the North Star. From there, narrow your attention to the touch of your breath—the sensation of it moving in and out of your body at your nostrils. Then focus on the rising and falling of your chest as your breath moves in and out. Then focus on the rising and falling of your belly. Choose one of those areas where you can anchor your attention on your breath; your belly, your chest, or your nose. Follow the breath into that part of your body, feel the breath there, and then follow it out.

Now follow your in-breath all the way in until it stops, and notice the stopping, notice the space between the in-breath and out-breath. Then follow your out-breath all the way out until it stops, notice the stopping, notice the space. In the space is stillness. The North Star sits still in the sky, and in between breaths that stillness resides in you. The North Star isn't perfectly still; it's almost still, just like your body as you follow your breath in and out to the place you have chosen as your anchor. Your mind is also not perfectly still. This is natural. You might notice that it wanders from your breath to other things like thoughts, emotions, memories, sounds, or other body sensations. When this happens, gently bring your attention back to your breath. The act of noticing your mind wandering elsewhere and gently bringing it back increases your capacity for mindfulness. If your mind wanders off every second, just bring it back every second. In this way, you build the stillness in yourself. With stillness, you gain more clarity and find your direction much easier. You can even expand your attention out to your whole body, imagining that it is the North Star, almost still; focus your mind on breathing in and breathing out from this expansive place.

Follow the in-breath and out-breath for five minutes.

Child Variation: Children can do one minute of North Star Breathing practice for each year of age. So a one-year-old can do one minute, a two-year-old two minutes, and so on.

Invite your child to put their hand on their belly and feel their belly rise as they breathe in, and deflate as they breathe out and see if they can find the stillness between breaths. If they are really distractible, and even a minute feels too challenging, you can try just three breaths. It's important to have a pleasant experience, so never press your children to practice; just ask them to try it and see.

The Train: Understanding the Railway to Progress

When I teach, I often talk about being on a train on the "railway to progress." I don't mean the old-fashioned kind of train with steam coming from the engines, rolling along at a pace where you can look out at the landscape and appreciate seeing a deer grazing peacefully in a meadow. That's a train you can breathe on. I'm talking about the sleek silver bullets of modern trains, careening down the train tracks at 150 miles per hour. Like the characters in Bong Joon-ho's film *Snowpiercer*, imagine the entire population of the planet on that train, placed in different cars. Some tell themselves they are content with the car they've been placed in. Some tell their children to work hard and get into a first-class cabin. Some push their way through the cars, doing whatever is necessary for a seat in the front. They want the cabin with the expensive linen tablecloths and silverware, or, better yet, a personalized sleeping car. They all focus on where they are inside the train. But what if I told you that the train was headed for the cliff? Would you try to get off, even if no one else did?

We are herd-like creatures. It is easy to just go along with things. We tell our children not to give in to peer pressure, but we do it all the time. If you try to go against the herd, people think you're crazy. You could say that our global civilization, which is heading toward any number of cliff edges like climate change or eco-catastrophe, is just like that class-stratified train of progress. I've heard things like, "It's too late to change course," or, "More harm will come to you if you don't go along with things." People even feel threatened and say, "To push on the brakes would slow down progress—and that is a dangerous thing," or, "It's not realistic."

Flying to the moon was not considered "realistic," but it happened. Stopping most international travel would have seemed impossible in 2019, but in 2020, it happened. The problem is that the train is going so fast that people can't get their bearings, no one even remembers where the brakes are, much less how the technology works. No one knows how to live outside the train car of our way of life. The most tragic thing about our civilization is that we can no longer imagine different possibilities. The hustle and bustle of daily living and entertainment distractions stop us from looking deeply into these kinds of thoughts should they arise in the first place. Our ability to envision a different life for ourselves has atrophied. Our global habit of favoring material gain above all else is the direct result of centuries of insensitive, colonial-industrial thought and action. When we talk about decolonizing our thinking, we mean to allow ourselves to think both around and beyond what is considered normal.

We all have vitality (life force) and it can't be snuffed out completely, just clouded over. Our society in the twenty-first century has mastered clouding over people's instincts and vitality. The very things we think help us—entertainment, drugs, processed food, business as busyness—are the very things taking us away from who we are, who our families could be, and, really, who the world needs us to be.

Society is currently designed so that the easiest thing for many of us to do is sit in front of an electronic screen. This helps us numb out and forget that we noticed something was wrong in the first place. Most of us don't notice we're on the train, and we certainly don't think about getting off, not even when we hear the train is heading toward a cliff. We might notice that the train is carrying a virus that is making us sick, yet we can't stop it. We numb our instincts and dull our abilities to connect with our deepest ways of knowing just so we can keep going. Sound like a dystopian novel? There's a reason big apocalyptic books, films, and TV shows are so popular among young people.

With this book I'm trying to grab you and tell you, *you must find a way to get off of the train, for yourself, for your family, for the future generations of the world.* This book is about protecting your family and guiding you all to a place of deep safety and peacefulness.

Since it appears there's no easy way off, we'll have to start with our imagination. Take my hand and imagine jumping. Dream with me and let's create an intention for your family that comes from your deepest-rooted wisdom. For that kind of powerful intention, let's invite your instincts to awaken.

Waking Up Our Instincts

In modern society, we don't hone our instincts, but we did just a few generations ago. For most of humanity's history this was an important practice, necessary for survival, leading to greater health and wealth for individuals and families. Today, our instinctual wisdom is something we trivialize or fear. There is a game called Peon that the American Indians of Southern California play, in which two teams of four players each face off against one other. A large blanket hides the playing team from their opponents. Hidden in the playing teams hand are white or black coyote bones. Songs are sung and players on the opposing team guess which colored bones are in which hands, once the blanket is dropped. Correct guesses win the team a *palito* (counter stick), which is thrown at their feet by the palito holder. There are fifteen palitos in all. Once a team wins all the palitos, the game is over. Today, it's easy to see it as a game of random luck, but it is actually a game of instinct.

Once I was working on an American Indian parenting project and a group of research scientists from the Oregon Research Institute came down for a conference to work with the tribal people. A game of Peon was set up—American Indians against scientists. The Indians beat the scientists in one of the fastest rounds I've ever seen. Peon can go on all night. This game was completed in less than an hour. One of the top scientists could be heard mumbling in the corner, "It isn't possible that they could guess and win that many times based on probability theory. It's against the odds." He didn't have the capacity to understand that it wasn't a game based on odds—it was based on instincts.

Our instincts are naturally rooted deep inside of our bodies, connected to an ancestral line that was strong enough to survive through insurmountable odds, and launch us into the world that we live in today. As far as artificial and sped-up industrial society is concerned, honing our instincts is a nuisance, but since *The Mindful Family Guidebook* is about what's best for our health and happiness as human beings and families, it is a vital practice.

The first step in understanding what is important for your family is identifying your core family values. This can't come from external markers of societies where families are falling apart and so many people are depressed. Did you know that the World Health Organization reported that in 2004 major depression was the third leading health problem in the world? They predict that by 2030 it will rank as the leading illness across ages and genders.

To understand what is important for you and your family, you have to rely on something more sacred and vital, something internal that is connected to your ancestral line, and for that you need to revive your instincts. Let's start with a practice to invite your instincts to awaken called a *walkabout*. For this activity, you will need to go outside, but first, read through the instructions below.

WAKE-UP OUR INSTINCTS WALKABOUT

Find a place outside to go for a walk, preferably a place with nature (with trees). For ten to fifteen minutes, walk and follow your instincts, let your body be your guide.

Direct your attention to your senses. Pay attention to the sounds you hear, the smells you take in, the feel of the wind or sunlight on your skin. Notice how you are on your own. Slow down, you're not trying to get anywhere. Notice your in-breath and your out-breath, and feel your feet on the ground.

In the morning you might notice the sunrise or the songs of the birds and feel inclined to follow the sound. At twilight, you might notice the softening of colors or the wind against your skin and feel inclined to walk where the wind guides you. Go in the direction that your instincts take you. Look at the sights around you as if you were seeing them for the first time. Let go of judgments or preconceived notions. If confusion or boredom or restlessness arises, notice it, but don't try to change it, just stay present to whatever you are experiencing with your senses without trying to change anything.

Notice inklings. If you don't feel anything at first, that's okay. You're planting the seeds, inviting nature to awaken your instincts. You can stop and wait until you feel an impulse to go in one direction or another. If your mind goes off to thoughts and planning or analyzing, notice this and bring your attention back to your senses, focusing on what you hear, see, feel, smell, even taste. Focus on each step touching the earth.

To further fire up your instincts, journal about your walkabout experience or share it with a close friend or family member. If you are doing this practice with your whole family, meet back in fifteen minutes and have a family sharing about something that stood out for you.

Family Free Write

In Stephen King's book *On Writing*, the author reflects on the impact of attention on the writer and their muse, "Your job is to make sure the muse knows where you're going to be every day from nine 'til noon or seven 'til three. If he does know, I assure you that sooner or later he'll start showing up." The things that we give attention to grow, and sharing your story is a form of attention; that attention will encourage the awakening of your instincts.

FREE WRITING

Once you return from your walkabout, take five to ten minutes and have each family member write or draw something from their experience. In free writing, you write without letting your pen leave the paper. If you can't think of anything to write, put that down on paper—*can't think of anything to write*—and continue that way until your next idea comes. If you are drawing and can't think of what to draw, simply scribble on the paper until an image comes.

Allowing for drawing or writing allows all ages to participate. Then give each family member a turn to share their writing or drawing if they choose. Let this be voluntary.

Your Child as a Mindfulness Bell:
An Informal Stopping and Noticing Practice

This practice is an informal training on stopping and noticing that you can do throughout the day. Before I learned this practice, stopping was one of the hardest things for me, and it's still challenging. I often work from home and I concentrate hard on what I'm doing. When my children come up to me, my habit is to not stop. I divide my attention by answering them while continuing to do work. This increases my stress level, and leaves them feeling only half-heard. They don't feel I'm really listening to them. And even though I know this, it is still hard to stop and listen fully.

In Thich Nhat Hanh's Plum Village tradition of Buddhism, there's always a clock with a chime in common areas such as the dining hall. Sometimes it's an old-fashioned cuckoo clock or a clock with a sound like Big Ben in London. Whenever a clock chimes, everyone stops to listen and take a moment to check in with themselves. They might focus on their breathing or just notice what they are in the middle of thinking, saying, or doing. I use my children's interruptions as my mindfulness chime, a bell that rings for which I have to stop doing whatever I'm doing, no matter what, so I can develop that habit of pausing and being fully present for whatever is happening for my child.

By conditioning, I am very achievement-oriented. The neural pathway I have now is very rigid and grooved out of years of concentrating and focus, which served me well in getting a PhD, but doesn't serve me in stopping and paying attention to the present moment and to what's most important. For that, I had to develop a new habit, a new pathway in my brain.

When I stop and break from my current habit, sometimes it honestly feels like loud shrieking static in my head. My habitual reaction is to resist being interrupted. So now, instead, I breathe and I notice my child asking for my attention. In that moment I may feel uneasy, but after a few moments of tuning in to my breath, I start to relax. How long it takes for you to feel at ease with this rhythm of stopping and breathing depends on how deeply your habit of not stopping is engrained in you.

First, before you start this practice, try the following simple Mindfulness of Sound practice with a chime or a bell to strengthen your ability to stop, notice, and enjoy the moment. It will help prepare you for Your Child as a Mindfulness Bell practice. It's also a good first practice to teach your children for developing the skill of stopping and noticing.

MINDFULNESS OF SOUND: INVITING THE BELL

For this activity, you will need a chime, bell, or tone bar.

Sit upright and comfortably together with your child. You might like to sit next to each other. Rather than "striking" the chime or the bell, Thich Nhat Hanh suggests you have the attitude of "inviting" the bell to make a sound, which makes the sound more beautiful. If you are doing this activity with your child, give them a chance to invite the bell once you have demonstrated how to do it.

Invite the bell to sound. Close your eyes and listen to it until you can no longer hear the sound. When you can no longer hear the sound, raise a hand in the air, and now notice the silence after the ring.

Ring the chime again and listen until you can no longer hear the sound and then raise your hand again, and listen to the silence.

Do this three times. Tune into how your body and mind are responding, and invite your child to do the same.

Your Child as a Mindfulness Bell: Every time your child comes to you, stop what you are doing, feel your breath wherever it is moving in your body, and notice your child as if you were seeing them for the first time.

You might notice that you feel a sense of calmness in stopping and listening. On the other hand, you might notice that you feel a sense of boredom or restlessness with this activity. All of these things are okay; what's important is *stopping and noticing* what it is to be alive in this moment. This quality of stopping and noticing is something we're going to practice a lot over the course of this year of transformation.

They say that it takes sixty days on average to develop a new habit. The skills we are developing are stopping and noticing and awakening our instincts. As with any skill, perseverance matters. And even more important than perseverance is having a sense of purpose or clarity about this new way of being together with your children and family members. That's where Family North Star Intention comes in. That's your motivation (your heart), and it will help you remember why you are on this journey in the first place. It will help you to get back on the path consistent with your true values when you get lost or have strayed. It will serve as a guide long after this book ends, protecting and nourishing you and your family to live a life most closely aligned with who you are truly meant to be.

CHAPTER 2

A FAMILY THAT LOOKS UP AT STARS CONNECTS TO ANCESTRAL ROOTS

Each star is a mirror reflecting the truth inside you.

—Aberjhani

In the next two chapters, you will ignite your instincts to complete the task of creating your Family North Star Intention. An intention is different than a goal. It's not something to accomplish, necessarily. It's more of a marker that steers you onto the right path and helps you find your way when you get lost, just like Polaris—the Star of the North. You will rely on your instincts to create your Family North Star Intention from a place deep within your bones, from a place connected with ancestral strength unique to your heritage. It may take you a month or two, or more, to be aligned with your intention. Because this is an evolving instinctual process, you might feel like you're climbing through the darkness at times, but if you stick with it, you will find clarity.

The ancient, natural world gives us a star guide that helped our ancestors find their way. This star that our ancestors gazed at sits in the sky for us as well. In the Northern Hemisphere it is the North Star, which in my language (Chippewa) is *Giwedanang* and it shines with a luminosity of 2,500 suns. It is the fiftieth brightest star, and it's easy to spot when the sky is clear. I want to share with you an ancient, mythical story of Giwedanang as told by the Paiute Indians of the Great Basin (Nevada, Oregon, California, Idaho, Utah, and Arizona).

In this story, a very brave mountain sheep boy named Nagah loves two things—to please his father and to climb tall mountains. One day Nagah finds a mountain he has never climbed before. It is the biggest mountain he has ever seen. He has never had such a challenge. It is hard to even find a way up. After many failed attempts, he finds a crevasse that goes down before turning up. Of course, he climbs into it. He feels happy. But on this day, there is a terrible rockslide. Nagah falls and scrapes his leg. Boulders come down on top of him. He becomes trapped inside, and he is scared in this dark place. When the rocks finally stop, he notices a light higher up the trail. Behind him is darkness. The rocks have blocked his way from returning. There is no way down; he can only go up, and so he does. He eventually gets to the most beautiful place in the sky. He feels so much comfort there and it is in this place that he dies, sort of. You see, his father, Shinoh, cannot bear to lose his son. His grief is overwhelming. When he sees his son up in the sky, he sends the power of his love, turning Nagah into the star that doesn't move—the North Star. His boy becomes a guide for all living things on earth and in the sky. His stillness is the gift.

The star of the north is actually not perfectly still, just almost still, while the rest of the northern sky moves around it. It aligns most closely with the north celestial pole and marks the way due north. On a clear night, face Polaris and stretch your arms sideways; your right arm points east, your left arm points west, and behind you is south. You have a guide and you are oriented. Your Family North Star Intention is meant to give you that kind of orientation, which you can always find your way back to, starting with North Star Breathing.

While we can always see Polaris on clear nights, when things are stormy, we can lose our direction. Storms happen in nature, and they also happen in families. Having a clear sky might even be an exception for some families. That's where North Star Breathing can help. It gives us an anchor that we can hold onto until the storms clear out of the sky so that we can see clearly and orient ourselves to living in alignment with our values. If we can clear the storms within our own minds and bodies, we can always get back on the right path, even if we've been going in the wrong direction for a long time, even if our minds have become so cloudy that it is hard to find our star.

It's important that it's our instinctual family star that we connect with. When we follow a false star, especially one given to us by an artificial society, we become sick. On the outside, things may look okay, but inside ourselves and inside our families, we know something is wrong. We feel out of balance. So we reach for more of the wrong things and get very busy, or we collapse into shame and we think that the thing that is wrong is us, and we stop chasing after anything except something that will make us numb, or give us a drop of temporary pleasure. We're trying to stop but in unskillful ways. Mindful breathing is much healthier for clearing the storm clouds.

Let's set an intention, an intention about leading your family on this journey. You're most likely the one who bought this book and are sharing it with others in your family, so at least initially, it will be your energy carrying the family forward through the different activities. You will be the family's heart—their motivation. It's important that you are clear in your mind about why you are doing this, even if initially that clarity is foggy and vague, like, "Something feels wrong," or "I know I need to do something." This intention should be strong enough to steady you through family storms that may arise.

A MINDFUL FAMILY YEAR: INTENTION SETTING

To practice with intention, light a candle and ask yourself, "Why am I taking this mindful family journey?" "Why now?"

Close your eyes and follow three breaths in and out. Then wait and see what bubbles up. Connect with your deepest intention. This will help guide you through the transformational year that is to come.

Write this intention in your journal, and also write it out to keep with you as a reminder when things begin to get busy, disruptions are happening in the family, and when you are facing resistance.

Remember, you are on a journey.

The Cairn: Markers of Core Values in Mindful Families

A cairn is an ancient way of marking a path used by cultures all over the world. It is a stack of stones used to indicate something important, like direction. To complete your Family North Star Intention, you and your family will need to build this cairn. You will collect information related to your heritage, examples of respect, and manifestations

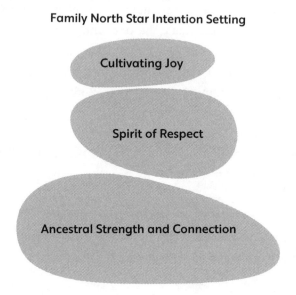

Family North Star Intention Setting

Cultivating Joy

Spirit of Respect

Ancestral Strength and Connection

of joy, which will be discussed. There are five maps that you will need to complete for this task. For each of these maps you will need to collect information: some you will already know, some you will need to research, and some you will have to rely on your instincts.

Stone 1 | Ancestral Strength and Connection

Your ancestors contain the foundations of your true nature. One October, years ago, I was at Deer Park Monastery in Escondido, California, and heard a talk by a Buddhist nun named Sister Dang Nghiem. It was a talk on fractals—never-ending patterns. It wasn't the first time I had come across this term in relation to family trauma, having heard it in a workshop related to somatic healing earlier that year, so my ears perked up. My understanding of the relationship of fractals to ancestors is inspired from Sister Dang Nghiem.

A fractal is a repeating pattern, and we can see examples of them everywhere in nature. If you look at a buckwheat plant, the kind that grows on the hillsides in Southern California, you will see that it splinters off into branches, and from there come more branches, and so on and so on. They repeat themselves. Like the buckwheat plant, you are also of a fractal nature, and you have repeating parts. Your cells are repeating patterns from your ancestors. Now, there are some things you may not want to repeat, like alcoholism, drug use, cruelty, and violence. Fortunately, through the way you live in the present, these things can be transformed so that you don't pass them down to the next generations. You need to remember all your ancestral patterns because it's important to know your challenges, and you have also inherited other qualities that are vital to manifest in the world, like courage, perseverance, curiosity, and zest. The world needs such qualities to continue. You will never find balance if you try to forget who you are and where you come from. You will feel like something vital is missing, and so will your descendants and the relations who come after you.

Remember how I talked about being on a train that I knew was headed for a cliff? Even with this knowledge, I struggled with making actions for myself or for my family that were consistent with what I valued most. Things seemed so complicated and fast, and I was largely responding to external societal forces. I was working all the time. I would be at my desk at four in the morning. This seemed normal. My grandmother began her day at this time. My mom sometimes worked triple shifts at hospitals as an emergency room nurse. These were patterns of survival for women that I witnessed growing up. My grandmother survived the Great Depression and got pregnant as a teenager. She had been in love, but my grandfather's family stopped the marriage. As soon as she had the baby, she had to leave my mom with her own mother and go to work in the city alone. My grandmother later married twice—to men that abused her—and had two more children. One husband moved her to California and then abandoned her with three children. He said he was going out for cigarettes and never came back. My grandmother got herself together after being left, and with some help, she got a loan, kept her home, worked as a waitress, eventually getting a steady job, and provided for her family.

As a child, I went on vacation every summer with my grandmother in a tiny little trailer. She had a great sense of adventure. She taught me that the best time to drive was when it was pouring rain and her best stories were about bears. I see my grandmother's sense of adventure and determination being repeated in myself and in both of my daughters. I moved to Sweden by myself at seventeen, Idaho at twenty-nine, and Oregon at thirty-two. I love traveling, I'm dedicated to my children, and storytelling is my passion. All of these qualities are built on the strengths of my grandmother. My grandmother was tenacious, and she also screamed when she got stressed. I developed her pattern of yelling and blaming when I am stressed. This is a habit I work to be aware of and transform in myself. If I don't transform it, it will continue in my children.

There is tremendous health and wellness to be found by connecting with ancient ways. When we connect back to our ancestors, despite trauma related to the creation of civilizations, we find health and vitality. Some of your strongest, life-sustaining family values are going to come from repeating patterns pulsating down your family line. They are going to come from long-ago ancestors, some of whom you've never even met, some of whom you don't even know.

Your ancestors live within you. It's my mother's undying optimism and appreciative joy that helped me to get my PhD at twenty-seven. It's as if she transformed all the abuse she witnessed growing up into kindness. And it is the Anishinaabe (Chippewa) first people ancestors passed down to me from my father that help me understand and continue to learn about my connection to the world. My father wasn't able to transform alcoholism brought on by historical trauma and colonization, yet the ancestral voices carried through him are the ones I hear most strongly. Over 90 percent of Indigenous people died as a result of first contact; for my dad to be here, laughing and with joy, is strength.

When we ignore our ancestral strength, it contributes to our being out of balance and disconnected. We are all fractals. We are all a continuation of our ancestors. Focus on the things that you want to carry forward for yourself, your children, your grandchildren, and so on into the next seven generations. We will talk about transforming things that you do not want to carry forward in later chapters.

Mindful families value ancestral strength and connection. Your Family North Star Intention has to do with life-sustaining values, which determine your direction, your priorities, and how you spend your energy. These values should not come from media, neighbors, or other external sources. They should come from your ancestral strengths and be at the core of who you are. You'll find these strengths through connecting with your instincts. You don't have to get this perfect for it to be effective, and it can be changed and modified. Acknowledging your family line, instinctually identifying ancestral strengths, and expressing important family values will speak to you in stronger ways over time (if you pay attention and tell the stories). This life-sustaining Family North Star Intention will protect and nourish your family.

Let's do some activities that get you in touch with your ancestors. Ancestors can have passed on or be living. They can be people you know and also people you have never met. Your ancestral lineage goes all the way back to the beginning of your people who knew the stories connecting you to the land—stories you likely have never heard.

Start with the Identifying Ancestral Strengths Instructions practice below and begin the three maps and warm-up activity included at the end of this chapter on page TK (Family Tree Map, Family Origins Map, Ancestor Continuation Map and Family Values Warm up) based on what you know right now.

Over the next year, you will add to this knowledge as you research your family genealogy and ancestral origins. Explore what was happening historically in the times and places your ancestors lived, and also go back to the ancient stories, myths, and legends of the regions where they lived. Most family trees go back three or four generations and get lost when you can no longer find linkages to people. With a generation usually comprising twenty-five years, this means that many of us can trace our ancestors by about a hundred years or so. I encourage you to research history and story as far as you can, all the way back to your earth-connected ancestors. We all have indigenous roots if we go back far enough. Look for the old stories of the land. Some of this you may find from interviews, in historical records, or from researching history and talking to storytellers, and some of it you will have to instinctually imagine.

Let me give you an example of discovery that came from instinct and story. My mom's family has Scottish roots, of which I knew nothing about until recently. I have been drawn to Scottish land since first randomly traveling there in my twenties. I stayed in Scotland for three weeks and didn't want to leave. I went back for my honeymoon and then again with my children several years ago, still not knowing I had any Scottish heritage. I was at an International Arts Festival in Scotland and went to hear a Scottish storyteller. He told the story of the Beira, Queen of Winter, goddess of all goddesses. I found this story by following my instincts and came to find out only recently that a majority of my mother's ancestry is from that region. The story of the Winter Queen is a story for another time but my discovery is an example of how following your instincts can lead to deep roots. The story of the Beira helps me manage the fierceness that comes to me through my mother's line.

If you know nothing of your roots, look to the land and the stories that captivate you most. Over the next year, see if you can go all the way back to the creation stories and mythology of these earth-connected ancestors who knew how to endure. They survived much longer than any modern generations and possessed strengths that we carry in our DNA today.

Before, after, and during the time you are completing your Family Tree Map and Family Origins Map, you may like to practice the Ancestor Visualization below.*

ANCESTOR VISUALIZATION

Stand in an upright, comfortable position. With your feet firmly rooted to the ground, imagine your head being gently pulled up by a string. Roll your shoulders back and down. We are going to go on a time traveling journey to the past.

Look at your right hand. Say to yourself, "This is my hand, and this is also my mother's hand." Look at your left hand. Say to yourself, "This is my hand, and this is also my father's hand."

....
* Adapted from Sister Chan Khong, 1999, "Touching the Earth Teaching," Mindfulness Retreat, University of California, Santa Barbara.

Close your eyes and feel your in-breath and your out-breath, noticing three complete breaths. Imagine yourself as having roots reaching backward, in a branching triangular pattern, one root attaching to your mother, and one root attaching to your father.

Imagine the root going to your mother. Picture her as she is now, or as she was when you were a child. If you did not know your mother, hold a space for her and see what comes up from your imagination and instincts. Don't evaluate or judge what happens, just trust your instincts. Bend down and touch the earth. (If bending is difficult, you can remain standing or sitting.) There are things you want to carry forward from your mother and other things you may want to transform. Notice the things that you want to carry forward. Her strengths.

Thank your mother for the gifts she has given you. When you are ready, stand back up.

Now look again at your hand and say to yourself, "This is my hand, and this is also my father's hand." Close your eyes and notice your in-breath and your out-breath, noticing three complete breaths. Imagine the root going to your father. Picture him as he is now, or as he was when you were a child. If you did not know your father, hold a space for him and see what comes up from your imagination and instincts. Don't evaluate or judge what happens, just trust your instincts. Bend down and touch the earth. (If bending is difficult, you can remain standing or sitting.) There are things you want to carry forward from your father and other things you may want to transform. Notice the things that you want to carry forward. His strengths.

Thank your father for the gifts he has given you. When you are ready, stand back up.

Repeat this process with your mother's mother, your mother's father, your father's mother, and your father's father. You can take as long as you like, or if you like, you can set a timer (perhaps for two minutes) for each ancestor.

Each time, remember to look at your hand. Say to yourself, "This is my hand, and this is also my grandmother's hand." Close your eyes and notice your in-breath and your out-breath, noticing three complete breaths. Imagine your ancestral root going from yourself, to your mother, to her mother (altering the people as appropriate for each ancestor). Touch the Earth. Each time take two minutes or so to connect with that ancestor. You can go back as far as you want to. If there are ancestors you do not know, hold a space for that and see what bubbles up in your imagination. It does not have to make sense.

In your journal, write down the strengths that come up for you at the end or after each ancestor. If nothing comes up for you at this time, that is okay. You can revisit this later.

Now choose either your mother's or your father's ancestral line to go further back. Go back to the beginning of these people following the same process. Where did they originate? Maybe you've heard stories. Maybe it is more than one place. Pick one. Maybe it's just a hunch. Start with the place you feel the most curiosity about or pull toward. If you don't feel anything, just pick a point of origin that you know. Allow yourself to be uncertain and still follow your instincts. If nothing comes up for you at this time, that is okay. Stay curious. You can practice this at different times with different ancestors.

When you are finished, put the qualities and strengths you have identified on the Ancestor Continuation Map.

Child Variation: You can lead your children through a modified version of this exercise with parents and grandparents, focusing on qualities they love about each person. Have them record what they discover in their journal.

Stone 2 | The Spirit of Respect

Minadandamowin is one of the first Chippewa words I taught my children. It means respect. An ancient wisdom teaching comes from the Seven Grandfather's Gifts of the Anishinaabe (Chippewa): "To honor all creation is to have respect." We call this the Spirit of Respect, and it is a central value in mindful families. To understand this kind of respect—honor for all of creation—you have to understand the concept translated by Indigenous people as "all my relations." In my language we say *nindinawemaaganidok*—meaning a profound form of interconnectedness.

One of the most valuable things that mindfulness has gifted me with is the felt sense of respectful relationship with myself, other people, and the larger universe. When we practice mindfulness, there are actually areas in the brain that correspond to this indigenous concept—self to self, self to other, and self to the universe. When these areas light up and join together, they fire up the well-being center of our brain and we feel happy and connected. The Spirit of Respect is the bond holding mindful families together.

My husband is a Cahuilla Indian from Southern California. When the Cahuilla make baskets in the traditional way, they sing and pray over those baskets. They are mindful of the thoughts they hold and the words they speak while they are making those baskets, while their attention is focused on the weaving. When the basket is finished, it is more than just a basket; there is a spirit that is woven into it. It is the same way with our interactions with our children. When we act in respectful ways to ourselves, to our children, to other family members, we are weaving the Spirit of Respect into our family, strengthening our bonds.

My husband honors me in our everyday lives by cooking, driving, parenting, and being there. He allows me space to write. I couldn't have written this book without his support. This book was written from his efforts, as well as from mine. I may have written the words, but my family, friends, and teachers provide the support and experience that are embedded in the pages.

When we honor our children, we create seeds of happiness in them that come back to us in the form of a happy family. How does the Spirit of Respect show up in your family? How do you want it to show up?

To look deeply into this, take ten minutes and complete the Spirit of Respect Map at the end of the chapter. Remember, what you give attention to grows. Genuinely give attention to the Spirit of Respect— really take the time to do this. Find a way to symbolize this respect in material form; you may like to reflect this respet in a personal item that you can carry with you or place in a prominent place in your home. You will need this personal item to ground you to the Spirit of Respect as you go through this journey.

North Star Breathing and the Spirit of Respect will orient you and keep your family bonds strong. These are anchors to come back to over and over.

Stone 3 | Cultivating Joy

Joy is strong happiness. It can look like laughter, smiling, or even crying (tears of joy). When I was a little girl, I wanted to be with my dad more than anything and I think that was because of his joyfulness. He was always smiling and could find the humor in any situation. His most commonly asked question to me was, "Are you serious?" as if that was the last thing anyone should be. He found joy in many things, including me.

My dad wasn't joyful because he had an easy life; he was joyful because joy makes life more bearable. We need joy to balance the suffering. Laughter is very good medicine.

The Navajo people have a teaching about a baby's first laugh as being a decision to stay in this world and connect with the community. When we laugh with someone, we feel more connected, it's good for both our physical and mental health, and it's an important survival skill for us and our children. Joy doesn't have to be something we wait for; it's something that we can cultivate now.

When was the last time you felt joy? When was the last time you laughed with your family, not at someone else's expense, but in a good way? Spend the next week and notice what brings you joy and, important, write them down. The act of recording will help you be aware of your joy.

On page TK, we'll learn how to create an actual map that will point to the many ways you develop the skill of laughter and joy. Each night before bed, write one to three things down on your Cultivating Joy Map (see page TK) that made you feel joy (or at least brought the beginnings of a smile). If you can't find anything, write things that have made you smile at other times in your life.

To cultivate joy, start by noticing what makes you smile. These are the things that you want to be sure you allow into your life, and to stop and notice them when they happen. You have to pay attention for at least ten to fifteen seconds for the joy to get into your emotional memory and serve as good medicine. Doing this on a daily basis waters the seeds of joy in you. Once you have watered them in yourself, you can water them in others and also share joy together as a family.

You may also like to complete the Visualization on Joy practice below.

VISUALIZATION ON JOY

Think of a time when you were happiest. What were you doing? How did that feel in your body?

Think of a time you laughed with someone. How did that feel?

If you have a hard time coming up with something, imagine something that could make you happy, imagine something that could make a family member happy.

In the next week, notice things each day that bring you joy; record five to ten of these things on the Cultivating Joy Map by the end of the week.

Child Variation: Lead your children through this exercise and have them record what they discover in a journal or share it with you in a story.

We have mapped out the cairn of your mindful family, touching on the three core values—ancestral connection and strength, the spirit of respect, and cultivating joy—necessary to complete the first stage of your journey: the Family North Star Intention.

Family North Star Intention Cairn

There are countless demands from society that will pull you in many directions. Knowing your own family values will help clear the clouds and lure of entertainment stimulation, numbing, addictions, and other distractions so that you can feel your instincts, find your Family North Star Intention, and know which way to go.

The Seven Grandfather's Gifts brought balance to a community when it had gone askew. It was a gift to them in terms of how to live in a way that resulted in harmony and sustainability. These seven teachings are reflected in the cairn on page 30.

These seven teachings are examples of a North Star Intention, pointing to how to best live in balance and harmony. Now it's time for you to create your Family North Star Intention Cairn. There are four steps involved in selecting your intentions: Choosing, Clarifying, Creating, and Uniting.

1. Choosing

Begin with the foundational values of ancestral strength and connection, spirit of respect, and cultivating joy. These three core values form the foundation of the Mindful Families cairn. In this activity, you will clarify how these core values fit for you and also add values unique to your family.

Foundational Stones

Ancestral Strength and Connection Stone #1. First reflect on the gifts that you want to carry forward from your ancestors. Review the Ancestor Continuation Map from the Ancestor Visualization on page 23 for values that you want to continue.

Spirit of Respect Stone # 2. Reflect on how your values reflect honor and respect among family members. Review your Spirit of Respect Map for how you symbolize respect within your family.

Seven Grandfather's Gifts

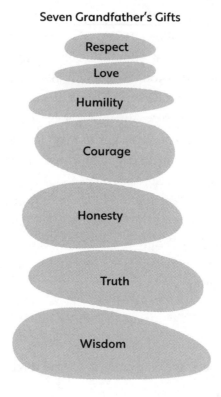

Respect

Love

Humility

Courage

Honesty

Truth

Wisdom

Cultivating Joy Stone #3. Review your Cultivating Joy Map. Reflect on how joy can be cultivated in your family.

You will use these reflections to identify your family values, which you will then craft into your Family North Star Intention Cairn. After reviewing these three maps, spend the next fifteen minutes journaling about what values are important to you for your family. It doesn't have to be perfect and it doesn't have to be final. This will be something that unfolds over time. Trust that the vision is already within you and your family members. List your values on the Family Legend.

2. Clarifying

Now that you have a list of foundational Family Values from the Choosing process, get specific and describe how that value can be expressed. For example, if a family value is kindness, what does that look like? Is it sharing, saying nice words, offering a smile, giving a friendly greeting? Clearly define your family values using the Family Values Legend at the end of this chapter. On this legend you will notice the three core Mindful Family Values for you to break down into behaviors. For example, Ancestral Strength and Connection can look like telling family stories, researching family history and putting it into a book to share, and/or learning and practicing cultural traditions together. If you are doing this on your own and bringing it to your family, share with them the core foundational values and have each family member complete their own Family Values Legend.

3. Creating

Once you've broken your values down into observable behaviors in the Clarifying process, each family member will create their own Family North Star Intention Cairn (See Family Vision Cairn activity). There will be three paper circles representing the three foundational stones, as well as additional circles reflecting other values family members bring. Family members will craft a collage of pictures, drawings, words, or images of symbols reflecting family values important to them. Some of the values will fit onto the foundational stones; for example, if a value is adventure, that could be put onto the cultivating joy stone. This cairn will be your Family North Star Intention that you will use for the next year on your journey to becoming a mindful family.

4. Uniting

This part of the process will take place over the next year. It involves taking this cairn with its individual circles and creating a mindful family star. The star can contain pictures, images, words, or drawings that capture the whole of your individual family members' values. This creation will be your Mindful Family North Star Intention crest.

FAMILY VISION CAIRN

Put on music in the background while doing this activity, which may take an hour or two, music that you all enjoy. You could put together a playlist of songs that all family members have selected together.

For this activity you will need an assortment of collage and art supplies, for example magazines or pictures, drawing paper, markers and pencils, glue, and scissors. You can even use paint. You will also need strong cardstock poster paper cut into circle shapes, representing stones to place your images on. You will need three large circles representing the three stones of ancestral strength and connection, the spirit of respect, and cultivating joy. You may also want to have one circle at the top for a photo of your family.

Individually, look for images that capture the values you have identified as important. Holding your family vision in mind, go through pictures or magazines and tear out images that resonate with you. Trust your instincts. You may not use them all. Just pull out whatever calls to you and put them to one side. You can also create your own drawings or download things from the internet.

Once you have all your images, go through the pile and ask yourself what the picture represents for you and if it fits with your family values identified on your legend. Even if you're not sure what it means, but it calls strongly to you, put it there; clarity about the image will come in time.

When everyone has their images, meet together and paste them onto the circles. You will have the three foundational circles (ancestral strength and connection, spirit of respect, and cultivating joy) that images can be pasted onto and then you can make additional stone circles if there are other categories you'd like to include. Link the circles together (you can fasten the circles together with tape, glue, string, or sew them on, etc.) so they make a line going down in the shape of cairn. All family members can paste images onto the foundational circles.

Once this is complete, have family sharing time about what the images mean and give examples of how those values are expressed. You could do this over several months, each time selecting a different image.

Put your Family North Star Intention Cairn in a place where family members can see it on a regular basis. As a family, create a place in your home, like an altar on a table or shelf in the living room where this cairn can be displayed and serve as a reminder of your direction as a family. Your intention is meant to be alive within your family; it is important to nourish and tend to the seeds that you are cultivating in yourself and other family members. To help in planting, watering, growing, and strengthening these values a Mindful Family Values Growing Log is included for this chapter. Each night you may find it helpful to log what seeds were planted or watered for the day, as well as your intentions for the next day.

Sharing | Storytelling Family Values

For thousands of years human beings sat around fires and told stories. Some of these stories were about family. That is how we keep our ancestors alive, through stories. Today, we have pictures we pass around, and maybe written on the back, if we're lucky, is the name of the relative. What's missing in these pictures often is the story of who these people are, and how we carry them forward and keep them alive in ourselves and in our children.

Family stories help shape children and impact who they become. "You're from a strong family," "A proud people," "A loving heart." With your storytelling, think about the main thing you want to portray. What is the value being taught in the story you are telling yourself and your children about who you are and where you come from? Bring in details, specific elements, and sound effects. In this way you are also revitalizing the oral tradition. If you don't know the full story, research, journal, and imagine what it would have been like to live in that time period. Even small events can reflect big values.

Repeated family stories can be as simple as the time you skinned your knee as a child and someone was kind to you, or a time an ancestor persevered through a daunting challenge, or something wise someone once said. When I was eleven years old, an old man on a park bench asked me what I wanted to be when I grew up. I said an obstetrician or a doctor, but maybe I wouldn't do it because it was so many years of school. He said, "What else are you going to be doing?" That simple phrase stuck with me and the time to get my PhD suddenly seemed insignificant. I was going to live those years anyway. I might as well do it learning about something I was interested in that would give me more choices about how I wanted to work in the world. It is a story I share with my daughters when they look ahead to the years of college. Use the Family North Star Intention Cairn to select a value to tell a story about a time that you experienced or saw someone manifesting a family value.

STORYTELLING

Sit in a circle, light a candle in the middle, and make a dedication to your ancestors. You can say, "We dedicate this time together to all our relations including all those who came before us and whom we are a continuation of. We live because they lived."

Take turns going around the circle having each person share a story about a family value from one of the images on the Family North Start Intention cairn. If you can express that value as a story of a family member, that is great, but it doesn't have to be at this point. Just tell about a time they experienced or saw that value expressed.

In sharing stories about family members, remember to practice the Spirit of Respect. While one person talks, everyone else listens; and share stories of family members embracing their strengths.

End the story time with each person saying one word that stands out for them of the stories they heard.

Finish storytelling with the North Star Breathing practice. For younger children, remember to shorten the practice (one minute of mindfulness for every year of age).

Blow out the candle.

Instructions for Identifying Ancestral Strengths

You will need the Family Values Warm Up, your journal, and three maps: Family Tree, Family Origins, and Ancestor Continuation and Transformation.

Your Family Tree Map

If you know your family history, start your Family Tree map. Give each person a place on the map and room to write in details about them. You can add squares for males, circles for females, and stars for nonbinary family members.

Our Family Tree Map

FAMILY NAME: _____

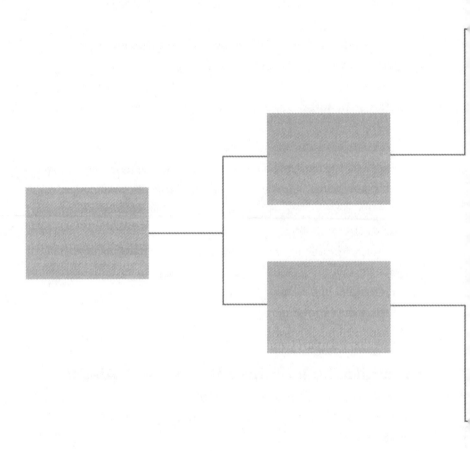

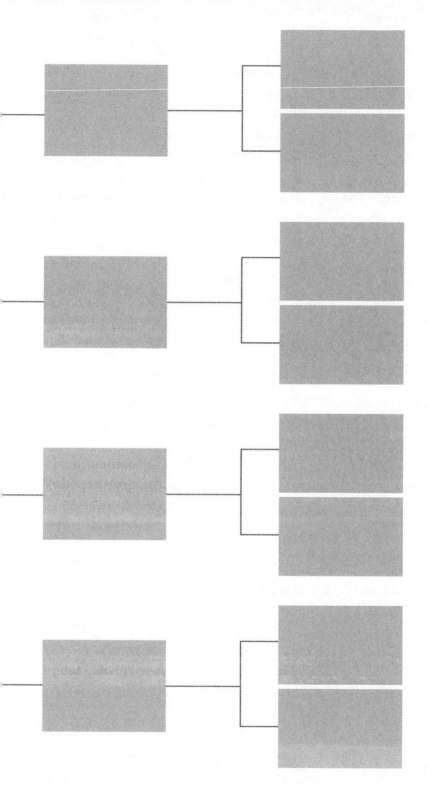

Fill in the name and gender of your family member, record their birth and death date, and fill in their country of origin as far back as you remember. (If they were born in England, for example, and moved to the Americas, write England and then put America in parentheses.)

Draw lines between married and divorced individuals and include remarriages. You can add branches for siblings going out from the side. You may find you have a many-branched family tree. If you do not know your heritage, start to research.

Complete Your Family Origins Map

Fill in the Family Origins Map below based on what you know now. You can expand on this as you research your family history. Ancient connections may become alive again as you begin to become more like earth-connected people who knew the stories of their land connections. Fill in the Family Origins Map based on what you know now. If a relative originated in France and now lives in America, put France with America in parentheses. You can expand on this as you research your family history.

Research and identify historical events that occurred for grandparents, great grandparents, or great-great grandparents. Keep going back. (Some of you may have to imagine to begin with; some things you'll know for sure.)

- Talk to relatives.
- Research records on family members.
- Research your family name.
- Research historical events that happened at the times your ancestors lived. At the time of writing, we are living in a pandemic. Do you have ancestors you don't know who also lived through a pandemic? What about wars, famines, times of great peacemakers?

Go back to the first peoples, the original inhabitants of the lands, and find their stories. Sometimes these are stories collected as folk tales, sometimes they are in ethnographic or anthropological records, and sometimes they come from interviewing people. Keep these collections in your Family Story notebook.

From these historical records, stories, interviews, and your own instincts, identify strengths/qualities/values of these people, your people, that you want to carry forward. Be sure to share these stories with your children so they are remembered and passed down.

Our Family Origins Map

FAMILY NAME: _____

Early origins of father's family line	
Origins I know about	*Origins I imagine*

Early origins of mother's family line	
Origins I know about	*Origins I imagine*

Complete the Family Values Warm Up

Your values determine your direction, your priorities, and how you spend your energy. Circle the twenty most important family values from the following list. Others may be important as well, but use your instincts and circle the twenty that speak to you most.

Our Family Values

Love	Loyalty	Friendship
Connecting with nature	Connecting with animals	Culture
Kindness	Respect	Healthy humility
Learning	Wisdom	Education
Peace	Stability	Relaxation
Adventure	Creativity	Free Time
Honesty	Integrity	Responsibility
Safety	Freedom	Travel
Calmness	Spirituality	Morals
Success	Power	Wealth
Autonomy	Fairness	Connection
Joy	Humor	Fun
Popularity	Strength	Leadership
Trust	Patience	Courage
Compassion	Balance	Competency
Challenge	Growth	Happiness
Self respect	Reputation	Service
Authenticity	Beauty	Generosity

Ancestral Visualization and Ancestors Continuation Map

Practice the Ancestor Visualization on page 23 and list your family's ancestral strengths on the Ancestor Continuation Map below. These are things you want to continue in the family line.

From the Ancestor Visualization, choose the strengths and qualities you want to carry forward from your ancestors.

Our Ancestors' Continuation Map

Continuation (Strengths/Values)	Transformation (Traumas/Difficulties)

Discuss the Spirit of Respect

Have everyone talk about and define what respect means to them by filling in the ending to these sentences.

Respect is . . .

Respect looks like . . .

Fill in the ways you like to express the Spirit of Respect in your family.

Pleasant greetings	Acknowledgement	Listening	Doing what you ask
Spending time	Showing Empathy	Giving Compliments	Doing what you say you'll do
Sharing your things	Helping with a task	Taking an interest	Nice surprises (gifting)
Using "Is it good for me, is it good for you?" as a guideline in speaking	Seeing what's good in them, even when they don't	Talking about the good about each other	Putting aside your needs for someone else

Cultivate Joy

Complete the Cultivating Joy Map below and appreciate how much joy you have in your life..

Day	Things that brought me joy today

Family Values Legend

Select the most important values that you will use for your Family North Star Intention Cairn and record them on the Family Legend. Use your Family Tree, Family Origin, Ancestor Continuation, Spirit of Respect, and Cultivating Joy Maps to select these values.

CREATE YOUR FAMILY'S VALUES LEGEND

Using your five maps, pick eight to fifteen of your most important family values. List them in the left column. In the right column list specific behaviors that demonstrate those values. For example, if the value is joy, behaviors that could reflect that are laughing together, sharing something exciting with one another, and spending time together in ways that family members enjoy. The three foundational values are included.

Value	What the value looks like
Ancestral strength and connection	
Spirit of respect	
Joy	

Value	What the value looks like

North Star Intention Growing Log

I always find that recording the positive changes we make as a family benefits us and helps us see our direction—our North Star—more clearly, even when times are murky or dark. The purpose of keeping a log is not to create another to-do list, but to celebrate when we planted beneficial values in our lives and tended to them.

Planted: You demonstrated the value or set the conditions for the value to emerge. For example, if the value is respect, you modeled this value by deeply listening to what a family member was saying, or you set the conditions for the value to manifest by doing nice things for a family member over the day.

Watered: You observed the value in a family member and reinforced it. For example, you saw the value expressed and complimented the person, or let them know the positive effect it had on you, or gave them a treat (a special snack or extra story or game time).

North Star Intention Values *List family values you want to grow*	Planted *Demonstrated, or set the conditions for the behavior to emerge*	Watered *Observed the behavior and reinforced it*	Intention for tomorrow

North Star Intention Values *List family values you want to grow*	Planted *Demonstrated, or set the conditions for the behavior to emerge*	Watered *Observed the behavior and reinforced it*	Intention for tomorrow

Over the Next Year

Completing this stage of your mindful family journey may spark in you the curiosity to research and fill in your family tree in more detail. You may like to keep a Family Story Book and record stories of family members listed on the Family Tree, and stories of your cultural origin. Include folk stories and creation stories as you find them, as well as historical research, to create a rich, unique record of your family's roots, which will nourish your children's sense of belonging in the great family of life.

...

Congratulations, you have completed Stage 1 of the mindful family journey: Family Visioning.

CHAPTER 3

MINDFUL FAMILY CIRCLE

See the light in others and treat them as if that is all that you see.

—Dr. Wayne Dyer

A circle is a powerful structure that is repeatedly found in nature, such as in the sun, the moon, and the earth itself. It is also found across cultures and throughout mythological history. King Arthur's famed round table had no head; everyone sat together equally in the circle. Black Elk, Holy Man of the Oglala Sioux, said, "In the old days all our power came to us from the sacred hoop . . . and so long as the hoop was unbroken the people flourished." Imagine building this kind of circle within your family.

Having a successful Family Circle is like tending a garden with different kinds of plants. There are certain things that everyone needs like soil, sun, water, and space, but depending on the type of plant (or person), they may need these things in different amounts or in different ways. There are many different types of people, yet as society has advanced it has narrowed the varietals, favoring some, while pushing out others. To make matters worse, our society favors competition, which can make rivalry the norm and collaboration the exception.

The first time I tried a Family Circle, it began with a storm of one-upmanship between my two daughters and ended with one daughter running out of the room. To be honest, no matter how many times I tried the Family Circle, one girl always left. My daughters are less than two years apart and the sibling rivalry got worse with adolescence. They wanted one-on-one time but not all of us together. When I told them that our Indigenous elder said we are stronger when we come together in the circle, they actually threw out a Western statistic they had heard me cite at some point: "Siblings get into arguments once an hour on average. This is normal."

In the previous chapter, over the course of about a month, you completed Stage 1 of this guidebook and created a Family North Star Intention. This month you will build a container and weave those North Star values into the fabric of your family. You can think of the container that you are building as a basket that holds the shape of the Spirit of Respect. The reeds that make up that basket are respect, safety, and creative collaboration. The primary weaving technique that you will use are mindfulness-focused improv games! This basket creates the space for the Mindful Family Circle where the family can operate as an ensemble.

My daughters finally came back together in a circle, but it took our family becoming a basket in the form of an ensemble for a bigger purpose to create our family circle. *Ensemble* is a theater term used to describe a group viewed as a whole. A researcher at the University of Munster in Germany (Huffmeier 2010) discovered that Olympic swimmers who felt more indispensable performed better in group relays than they did in individual races. Feeling their efforts mattered for the group outcome was the key to producing motivation to perform well. My whole family became an ensemble when we acted together in a play written by my oldest daughter called *Menil and Her Heart* about missing and murdered indigenous women and girls.

This month you are setting the conditions for the family to come together as an ensemble, in such a way that each member is individually nourished, while still feeling indispensable to the whole. You need to dig below the surface and go beyond the offerings of society and statistics, just like you did when you made your Family North Star Intention. To do this, you need to continue to give space for your instincts and natural wisdom to emerge and guide the process for your unique family. For this month's instinct awakening practice, you will continue to go out on a wander, but this time from a sitting place.

WAKE UP OUR INSTINCTS: OUTDOOR SITTING PRACTICE
Go outside and find a place to sit and observe nature. This can be done in the city or the country. A yard or bench with grass and trees is a fine spot. Sit in this place and open up your senses.

Start with Mindfulness of Sound practice: close your eyes and open your ears letting the sounds come to you. Don't focus on what the sounds are, but rather the quality of the sounds (pitch, tone, vibrational quality). Listen to the sounds that are farthest away, then listen to the sounds that are nearby. Listen to all the sounds that you hear with curiosity. Next, feel the wind, sun, or cold against your skin. Rub the grass or dirt between your fingers. Activate your sense of touch.

Then, with a soft gaze, gently explore what you notice with your other senses, letting go of thoughts and letting your natural instinctual senses take in what is in the environment. Notice sights and smells.

Journal about this experience or share it with family members. If you are doing this with your whole family, meet back in fifteen minutes and tell stories about what you noticed.

So, what is a Mindful Family Circle? A family circle creates a formal space in which families set aside ritualized (sacred) time together in a circle to transmit the values set forth in the Family North Star Intention and learn to work together as a healthy ensemble. It can be as little as five minutes or as long as two hours, conducted monthly, bi-monthly, or weekly. This nourishing, protective environment provides opportunities to set aside time to strengthen family connections, cultivate family joy, plan and work toward family goals, develop important life skills (problem-solving, creativity generation, and healthy communication), establish family guidelines, and resolve conflicts.

I have taught the skill of family meetings with circle components in many settings, including in a family strengthening research project in Vancouver, Canada, with an aboriginal population with my colleague Betsy Davis. When we discussed introducing family meetings to the counselors, the lead therapist stated that this was an advanced skill and too difficult for many families. Given my experiences with my own family, you would think I would have heeded his advice and been content to never try this again. Instead, I rolled my eyes and pushed ahead with the family meeting, agreeing to a few preparation sessions where families could learn about healthy communication.

Stopping, Noticing, and Offering Kindness

In Chapter 1 Stopping and Noticing was introduced. Now we are adding the skill of offering kindness. The time we spend together should be steeped in kindness. It may seem magical, but science reports that six hours of conscious family time a week is the necessary ingredient for happy, healthy families (Graham & Crossan 1996). The more time children, particularly adolescents, spent with both parents during meals and other moments of family time, behavioral problems, substance abuse, and delinquent behavior occur less often, and academic achievement improves, as shown in higher math scores (Milkie, M; Nomaguchi, K., & Denny, K. 2015). In spite of how important family time is, a *Wall Street Journal* survey reported that 40 percent of respondents stated that a lack of time was a greater problem for them than a lack of money.

Family time can include time spent sharing interests, playing a game, and eating dinner as long as there is Spirit of Respect present and some of the times involve kindness and cultivating joy. One practice we covered last month that contributes to family time is Child as a Mindfulness Bell. This month we will add Mindful Family Circle and Finding the Treasure. We have been treasure hunting for ancestral strengths. This month we will hunt for things we enjoy in our loved ones through the Finding the Treasure Game, which will be this month's focus for Family Circle, so let's start there!

STOPPING, NOTICING, AND OFFERING KINDNESS: INFORMAL KINDNESS PRACTICE

Finding the Treasure

Designate a certain period of time (ten to fifteen minutes) each day to catch your loved one doing things you enjoy.

Erase all preconceived notions you have about them and notice all the things that you appreciate about them or their behavior in this moment, as if you were seeing them for the first time. Let them know the specific things you genuinely appreciate about them.

We spend a lot of time noticing what isn't working and glossing over what is. This kindness practice gives an opportunity to stop, notice, and offer kind words and gestures. It waters seeds of happiness in others. Think about kind words you can say to let your family members know that you appreciate them. Acknowledge small things—the sprout of something you appreciate—to encourage growth. Notice behaviors you like ("Thank you for putting your things away, it makes the house look nice"), as well as acknowledging their inherent jewels ("I feel so happy just being around you").

Stopping, noticing, and offering kindness are foundational skills for mindful families. They are a touchstone you can always come back to if things seem like they are going in a wrong direction and you don't know what else to do.

Simple Treasures

I like how you are sharing with your sister.	Thank you for cleaning up your mess.	I appreciate you doing what I ask.
I feel so happy when you tell me good morning.	It's so nice to spend time with you.	Your smile makes my day.
Your creativity is awesome.	That's so sweet that you helped your brother.	Nice job sticking with it, even though it's hard.
I appreciate you clearing the table.	It makes me happy to see you so happy.	I love your sense of humor.
Thank you for keeping the bathroom clean.	You have amazing concentration.	I really like how you come sit with me in the morning.

Family Circle Preparation: Offering Kindness

Prepare yourself for participating in a Mindful Family Circle with a formal practice that waters the seeds of kindness for yourself, as well as other family members, called loving kindness.

I first heard of this practice in a book called *A Path with Heart* by psychologist Jack Kornfield. I was on my way to Coeur d'Alene, Idaho, with my Golden Retriever, Thunder, to take a job as a reservation psychologist. I stopped at a friend's house in Coos Bay, Oregon, and the book was in his guesthouse. My instincts led me to memorize the practice, something I rarely did at the time.

May you be filled with loving kindness.
May you be well.

May you be peaceful and at ease.
May you be safe and protected both inside and outside.
May you be happy, truly happy.
May you be free.

I got to Coeur d'Alene just in time for winter. The day I arrived, a cold front had rolled in from Alaska. Being from California, I wasn't used to driving on black ice. The first time I hit the ice, I did a 360 and kept going. The second time I hit it, I slid into a field but was able to drive out and I kept going. The third time hitting the ice, I couldn't keep going. I was going downhill around a curve and my car started fishtailing. I remember the flares on the road and an ambulance down the hill (because someone else had also spun out). I don't remember my Isuzu Trooper going into the air, spinning around, and landing back on all four wheels. I do remember slamming into the embankment and everything finally becoming still. Before anything else, I turned to look over my right shoulder and saw the feet of my dog flying out the shattered window. I got out of the car to follow him, and the paramedics followed me. Thunder got to ride in the fire truck and I got a trip in the ambulance to the hospital.

The worst part of this experience was being strapped down on the table for what seemed like hours until the doctor could get to me. I had suffered a concussion. The next week I promptly returned to work and was sent back to the same hospital to see a patient. When I entered the hospital, my heart started to race, my breathing was shallow, and I felt clammy. I thought I was losing my mind. I went to the bathroom and instinctually recited the loving kindness verse to myself, over and over, until the symptoms decreased enough for me to talk to the patient. I later realized I was experiencing PTSD and these simple ancient phrases are what got me through it. You are going to learn this same practice before attempting a Mindful Family Circle.

STOPPING, NOTICING, AND OFFERING KINDNESS:
LOVING KINDNESS PRACTICE

Sit in a comfortable position with your spine straight but relaxed. If you are lying down, rest comfortably on your back. Begin by noticing your breath coming in and out of your body, not trying to change it, but allowing it to be as it is. Pick a spot to anchor your breath in your abdomen, chest, or nose. As you breathe in notice the in-breath and the sensations in the area of the body where you are anchoring your breath. Follow the out-breath out all the way to the pause. Continue breathing this way for several minutes.

Now picture someone or something that it is easy to wish good feelings for. This could be a child, an animal, even something from nature. Offer the phrases,

> *"May you be filled with loving kindness.*
> *May you be well.*
> *May you be peaceful and at ease.*
> *May you be safe and protected both inside and outside.*
> *May you be happy, truly happy.*
> *May you be free."*

Then imagine yourself, perhaps as a young child or now. Offer these same phrases to yourself,

> *"May I be filled with loving kindness.*
> *May I be well.*
> *May I be peaceful and at ease.*
> *May I be safe and protected both inside and outside.*
> *May I be happy, truly happy.*
> *May I be free."*

You can also make up your own phrases.

Continue to stay connected to your breathing, allowing whatever sensations, emotions, or thoughts to arise without trying to change them, letting go of the story behind them.

Next offer these phrases to someone neutral, someone that you don't know that well or have strong feelings for.

Then offer these phrases to someone that's difficult. Don't pick the most difficult person at first, just someone mildly irritating.

Finally offer these phrases to all beings in the world.

Child Variation: Picture a beloved family member or pet. Send them a few kind wishes, like, *"May you have such a happy day today."* Next, send the wishes to yourself, like, *"May I have a really fun and peaceful day."* Send wishes to a sibling or other family member. "May you be happy and feel loved." Finally, send the kind wishes out to the world, *"May all beings be healthy and safe."*

This practice can provide nourishment for you, help you connect with the love you have for family members prior to spending time together, stop you from saying things you will later regret, and help you to handle difficult situations in ways most consistent with your values.

Over time, if you can get other family members to take between five to ten minutes alone before the meeting to ground and center themselves, sending kindness out to each family member, that's great. If everyone is on board, you can do this together at the start of the circle. But start on your own before coming together with your family. You can record this, have someone read it to you, or listen to the loving kindness practice on the Mindful Families website.

Family Circle Building

Creating Respect, Safety, and Creative Collaboration

Creating the conditions for a Mindful Family Circle involves creating a safe container (space). When we feel safe, our thinking become more flexible and creative, and the social engagement parts of our brain become more accessible, which leads to increased empathy and kindness. Kindness is a necessary condition for safety to support a nurturing family environment for all members. When there is safety and kindness, then creativity can flow and true collaboration can happen. This is where the whole becomes more than the sum of its parts in a way that nurtures the whole as well as the individual.

Many families (when they come to the point of a family circle) have set down some pathways that provide the conditions for put-downs, conflict, and apathy. This isn't the fault of the family. In fact, many outside influences model and promote these kinds of conditions through emphasizing competition over cooperation, unkind speech, lack of empathy, too much busyness, and cutthroat business practices that we absorb every day through media and mainstream institutions.

Let me give you an example of conditions that create difficulty. My daughters were seeing a piano teacher for individual lessons. To motivate them, she would play them off one another. She would say to each sister, "Your sister does this better than you." This led to the girls not being able to play their instrument in front of each other without arguing and putting each other down. The teacher thought it would motivate them to work harder. She was trying to help, but rather than being engaged in the joy of piano and supporting one another, they pulled each other down. It made auditions worse and added more animosity to their relationship. Instead of motivation, like the teacher thought she was accomplishing, the girls worried what the other would think if they got an unfavorable evaluation. Their anxiety increased, their joy lessened, and they stopped playing piano.

What's most important when introducing a Family Circle is that it is a positive experience for everyone, and family members feel nourished through being part of the group (ensemble). Set the conditions for kindness to emerge among family members, even if it's just a drop of kindness. This may mean that you need to start out small (five minutes) to set up your family for success. You will have to be present and focused on Finding the Treasure to understand what each family member needs.

Family as Ensemble

Let's get down to the work of building the container of a mindful family ensemble with improv games.

The guidelines and improv games selected for the Mindful Family Circle all promote awakening instincts for health and well-being. They also promote respect (Make Each Other Look Good, Honoring Others), safety (Space for Mistakes, Sovereignty, Noninterference), and creative collaboration (Yes-And Attitude, Give and Take Climate, Share Your Gifts).

I first learned improv skills through games my daughters would bring home from the South Coast Repertory Theatre in Costa Mesa, California. Later I took improv classes and acted in a few plays. I discovered that improv can be a powerful practice of being in the present moment. Nothing gets me more focused than being on stage. If you aren't present, you can miss your line, you can't react to what's in front of you, and everyone is watching. And if being on stage isn't enough of a challenge, with improv you don't even have lines.

Improv skills help on the stage and they also help in life. When Google hires employees, they look for the ability to process on the fly (honing instincts), a willingness to relinquish power, ease with creating space for others to contribute (give and take), and the resilience to be able to learn from failure—all things that you practice with improv.

Building the Container (Weaving the Basket)

	Spirit of Respect Themes Guides	Weaving Technique *Improv games*
Respect opening and closing rituals	*Make Each Other Look Good*	*Loving Kindness Practice*
	Make Each Other Look Good Ball Pass	*Find the Treasure*
	Honoring Others	*Honor Circle* *Secret Gardener*
Safety guidelines	*Noninterference*	*Mindful Listening/ Speaking* *Rocking Practice*
	Sovereignty	*Right to Pass*
	Space for Mistakes	*Mistake Performances*
Collaboration intention	*Yes-And Attitude*	*Picnic Planning*
	Give and Take Climate	*Give and Take Game*
	Share Your Gifts	*What's Missing*

Building the Container

1. Respect

So much of our society is filled with the critic, people criticizing each other or themselves. Television and movies are filled with putting someone down to get a joke; and we all laugh at the other person's expense. John Gottman, a famous marriage researcher, identified four relationship destroyers. He calls them "the four horsemen of the apocalypse." These horsemen are criticism, contempt, defensiveness, and stonewalling. He can predict if people will get divorced or not with 90 percent accuracy just from observing them in a room and watching for the presence of these four things.

Making each other look good and honoring each other is a form of respect. It's what Dr. Wayne Dyer describes as, "Seeing the Light in others and treating them as if that is all that you see." People will rise to be more than they could be when their strengths or potentials are highlighted in someone else's eyes.

To promote respect, begin with ritualizing the space. A circle symbolizes equality. There is no one higher and no one lower, every member is equally important. Arrange a sitting area in a circle where all members can see each other. It's best to have a ritual for starting and ending the circle such as lighting a candle, ringing a bell, or saying special words.

Below are five rituals that can be used inside and outside of the circle to grow these seeds of respect.

Opening Ritual | Loving Kindness Practice

Do this beforehand, or as a start to the family circle, to set the conditions for embodying the Spirit of Respect. Work up to having siblings send kind wishes to each other and be sure to include yourself in this. Setting the conditions to make each other look good starts with how we treat ourselves.

Informal Practice | Finding the Treasure Game

To water the seeds of seeing the light in others, play the Finding the Treasure game. Plan a designated time each day to observe your loved one. Erase all preconceived notions that you have about them and notice with fresh eyes all the things that you like about them or their behavior in this moment. Let them know the specific things you appreciate as these details matter.

Informal Practice | Secret Gardener Game

Family members each have a jar with their name on it in a designated place that everyone can see. Each family member is secretly assigned to another family member as their gardener. Every day for a week they have to water the flower (write something they noticed the family member doing or something they appreciate about the family member and secretly put it in their family member's jar). At the end of the week the jars are opened and read privately or aloud. After a week members can rotate.

Informal Practice | Make Each Other Look Good Ball Pass Game

To start small, introduce Mindful Family Circle enthusiastically with a five-minute game of Making Each Other Look Good Ball Passing where winning is the number of passes the group makes, ending the circle while everyone is having a pleasant experience. A special light-weight beach ball is good for this game ("I got this great ball and I want to see how many times we can gently pass it to each other in five minutes without talking." Or "Let's see if we can beat last week's score.").

Closing Ritual | Honor Circle

To reinforce this quality of making others look good, share an Honor Circle. In a circle, each family member says something they appreciate about the person to their left, one at a time, until the honoring goes all the way around the circle, ending with an appreciation given to the first person who spoke. This is great way to end the Mindful Family Circle.

2. Safety

Safety is established through practicing mindful speaking and listening skills, sovereignty, and resiliency after making mistakes.

Mindful Speaking and Listening

Respectful communication is a primary way of transmitting the Spirit of Respect. Mindful Speaking and Listening is a stopping, noticing, and offering kindness practice. There are two formalized ways of communicating in Family Circle: Talking Stick, also known as "talking piece." For this month's circle, you are going to work with the Talking Stick.

Talking Stick

A talking stick is a staff used by many American Indian tribes to pass around the circle to take turns to speak, allowing every member of the circle to express their point of view. For this month's practice, you are going to make a Family Talking Stick.

FAMILY TALKING STICK

Making a Family Talking Stick is done in two parts: gathering of materials and creating the stick. To gather materials, go on a walkabout in nature, individually or with your family together, to find a stick thick enough to hold in your hand. Also find items as simple as paint and a feather, or more elaborate items like stones, shells, or other materials. Each family member can contribute items meaningful to them. These decorations are then attached to the stick.

To create the stick, the family comes together with each person contributing. Family members can collaborate on an overall plan for colors and where items go, or the stick can be divided into equal sections, with each family member taking turns decorating their section of the stick as they wish. The Talking Stick is going to be an important part of your family circle.

Mindful Listening

There is a Chippewa word *manajiidiwin*, "they respect each other."
This is the idea we bring to mindful listening: to treat someone with
care. We have two eyes and two ears, but only one mouth, yet many of
us don't listen well. We channel the information we hear into how it
relates to us and go off on a story in our own minds, plan what we're
going to say next, evaluate what we just said, or get lost in thoughts
completely unrelated to what is being communicated. Mindful listening involves being present and listening to the information being
spoken to you with your full attention. When you notice your mind
has drifted off, take a breath and return your attention to listening.
Building mindful listening skills is critical for a healthy ensemble.
When things get rocky, go back to more listening and less talking.

Mindful Speaking

The Chippewa word *Zoongide'ewin* means "strength of heart."
American Indian storyteller Leslie Marmon Silko says, "Where I come
from, the words most highly valued are the words spoken from the
heart, unpremeditated and unrehearsed." Mindful speaking aligns
us with what the universe wants, our true path, the path with heart.
With Mindful Speaking, stop and feel your feet on the ground, feel
the rhythm of your breath, and connect with your heart. Slow down.
From this place you will speak. In speaking you consider, "Is what I
have to say good for me? Is it good for you?" and "Is it true and necessary?" This also awakens your instincts because you are talking more
from the heart and gut then from your head. Beyond the kindness
guidelines try not to judge what you say.

You can practice mindful listening and speaking with a storytelling
improv game called Storytelling Round.

STORYTELLING ROUND

For this game you are going to create a story, one word at a time. Sit in a circle, select a Story Starter that starts the story with "once" or "there" or any word they choose as long as it begins the story. The person to their left adds the next word, and so on, with the next person always adding a word that adds to the sentence or begins the next sentence. Listen to the story that emerges, letting go of ways you want to craft the story, and letting the word that you contribute fit with what's come before you. The story ends when two players use the words "the" and "end," at a natural ending, or at a designated time.

We will focus more on difficult communication in the chapter on Family Peacemaking, but for now pay attention to speech so it is respectful and not hurtful to other family members. It is also important that stories aren't told that are embarrassing or hurtful to others, but instead make each other look good. Seeing the best in each other, even beyond what they can see helps family members stretch to become their ideal selves.

Sovereignty

It is important to acknowledge the power we hold as a group, as well as the importance of each individual family member. We call this individual power *sovereignty*. It is a type of freedom. In the Circle, each family member is encouraged to participate and honor their unique gifts and to share them with others, but some may not be ready for this so they are granted the right to pass. This acceptance of non-participation can set the foundation for later participation and support the feeling of safety within the circle. People often get things out of listening even if they are not participating.

If there is a lot of sibling rivalry or family discord, members can be told they are all valued, and if they have difficulty sitting in the circle following the guidelines, they can take some time in an area designated for quiet wiggling, drawing, or mandala coloring. This area should be reserved for one person at a time. It's important not to frame this in a punitive way, but to give options for people's needs. This demonstrates the practice of removing oneself from the situation when necessary. It's also important to acknowledge developmental stages as infants and young children can't be expected to sit for long periods or to follow guidelines exactly. Allow leeway for them.

When another person is speaking, it is important to show respect and not interfere. Sitting still can be hard at times. Even adults can get agitated if they disagree or are uncomfortable with what another family member is saying. If this happens, they can stay present with a gentle rocking practice that can help them find balance among difficult emotions or heightened energy. Try it yourself before teaching others.

NONINTERFERENCE ROCKING PRACTICE

Sit quietly and take a deep breath. Feel your breath all the way in and all the way out for several breaths. Then gently rock to the right. If you have a lot of space, lean until you're just about to fall but can still balance. Notice all the sensations in your body that help with your balance and how it feels to be in this position. Then rock back slowly to center, paying attention to each sensation as you move back to balance. Then slowly rock to the left repeating this process without disturbing the person next to you. Do this as many times as needed until you feel ready to rejoin the group. When you are in a group, you can do this by subtly rocking left or right, being careful to not bump into the person next to you. Notice if you feel more present and able to pay attention.

Mistakes Resiliency

Something that stops participation and kills the process of creativity, openness, and safety in people and groups is criticism, perfectionism, and fear of failure (looking stupid). It's okay and only human to make mistakes. Creating an environment where it's okay to make mistakes, where mistakes are celebrated even as part of learning, and understanding that you will not be made fun of or seen as less than is necessary for families. The improv world helps to change this dynamic by making mistakes fun and teaching that mistakes are a stepping-stone to success. If you're not making mistakes, you're not really growing or learning. We can practice this with the I Made a Mistake game. I first played this game at the Interpersonal Neurobiology Conference at UCLA. The entire audience had to stand and take turns to announce "I made a mistake." And then cheer, "Wahoo."

I MADE A MISTAKE PERFORMANCE

Have family members say all together, "I made a mistake, Wahoo," and throw their hands up in a cheer. Do this several times as a warm up.

Now teach them the cheer, *"I took a risk. I made a mistake. I'm still here, Wahoo."* Arms up at Wahoo—and then bow. Practice this until everyone has it.

Now each member will go in front of the group and share a time, recently, where they made a mistake. They will tell it as a story and when they finish, they will end with "I took a risk. I made a mistake. I'm still here, Wahoo," and take their bow. Then everyone in the audience claps.

You go first to model it. Mistakes can be anything: "I smiled at someone and they looked away." "I burned the toast." "I said a joke and no one laughed." "I invited someone somewhere and they couldn't go." "I dropped my food on the floor."

3. Creative Collaboration

In creative collaboration the family works in an ensemble to build something bigger than the sum of its parts. It involves a "yes-and" attitude, giving and taking, and contributing what's missing.

Fostering a "Yes-And" Attitude.

At the same Interpersonal Neurobiology Conference on play at the University of California, Los Angeles, I saw the singer Alanis Morissette being interviewed. She said that to create her music she has to screen out all the naysayers and critics, and surround herself with people that support her art. In other words, "yes-and" people.

Have you ever noticed what happens when you come up with an idea and you're met with a no? The enthusiasm quickly seeps out of the interaction. Even a "yes-but" response is draining. But when someone responded with "yes-and" to everything, then there is magic. Now your creativity is flowing, your brain is opening up, ideas you may not have considered or even imagined start appearing. A "yes-and" attitude is vital for creativity, whether it is for family members to plan a family outing, solve a problem, or apply to a social situation.

Einstein said, "Imagination is more important than knowledge." Creativity and imagination are vital skills for operating in the world, which we want to water and grow in our families. A "yes-and" attitude is a way of practicing support, showing respect, and expanding what's possible. It also helps people feel good about themselves and one another.

"YES-AND" PARTNER PICNIC

Divide into partners for this activity, ensuring everyone gets a chance. It's important that no one is left out. The partners are going to plan a picnic.

In round one Partner B responds with a No to all of Partner A's ideas. In round two, Partner A responds with a "yes-but" to all of Partner B's ideas. In round three Partner B responds to all of Partner A's ideas with "yes-and," building on their partner's responses. Partners share with the larger family the picnic they went on with the "yes-and" scenario, and the challenges they experienced in the other rounds.

Give-and-Take Game

The Mindful Family Circle provides a space where everyone matters. Rather than having a few main stars, each member is indispensable. Family members are supported in equally stepping into the spotlight and then blending back out into the group. Both the Give-and-Take Game and the What's Missing Game train these skills.

Being able to give and take helps set the stage for healthy consensus building. Social psychologist Jay Hall found that consensus building, early on, produces more effective outcomes than groups that just focused on simple decision-making methods. It's important to spend time valuing each member's perspective and contribution as invaluable to the whole so that all family members can feel that they matter and are irreplaceable.

GIVE-AND-TAKE GAME

Stand in a circle. There can only be one person moving at a time. The person moving is the Taker. Everyone else is a Giver. Givers are frozen, watching, and listening. The Taker has to keep moving until someone else takes their spot.

When a Giver decides to become a Taker, they start moving. There is no talking allowed; this is all done nonverbally. Two people can't move at once, so as soon as a new Taker begins, the current Taker has to become a Giver.

If certain people dominate, you can divide the group in half with an audience and the players. Each player's time ends if only a few people dominate the scene.

What's Missing Game

In this game, players are required to notice what others are offering and add to it or change it, seeing how many creative images the group can make.

WHAT'S MISSING GAME

One person stands in the middle and strikes a pose. Another person guesses what they are and adds something. A third person goes in, taps one to leave and then adds something to the other person's pose to create something new.

Players keep rotating into the group to tap a person to leave and add something missing to the player standing.

These games should be played often to water the seeds that you have planted. Remember, a good director recommends needed changes in a way that respects the sovereignty of the actor's art (in this case, their life path), as well as wanting to empower the actor so their piece in the performance will energize everyone. Use the skills you are gaining from Finding the Treasure to notice what worked in your Mindful Family Circle and build on those things and not only focus on the difficulties.

Storytelling: Strengthening Ancestral Family Connections

We have more strength as a healthy, connected family than we do as individuals. Each of us is strengthened and can flourish when the hoop (or circle) is whole and connected. Last month we worked on getting in touch with our ancestral strengths. This month we will continue with sharing family stories using a talking circle format.

A talking circle is a tradition in many American Indian tribes. A Talking Stick is presented to the first speaker. Only the person holding the stick can speak. The speaker practices Mindful Speaking and uses the guidelines of "Is it good for me? Is it good for others?" Everyone else practices mindful listening. When the speaker is finished, the talking stick is passed to the left (clockwise) until it has gone around the entire circle.

For Family Storytelling, introduce a prompt like, "Tell a family story about something that someone in the family did that made you feel happy, or something that was kind." Follow the guidelines on the Family Circle: Family Storytelling Worksheet to conduct your Mindful Family Storytelling Circle.

MINDFUL FAMILY CIRCLE: FAMILY STORYTELLING
Family Circle Guidelines
- Honoring gifts: Participate and bring your positive presence.
- Noninterference: Rocking Practice is allowed if you feel wiggly.
- Sovereignty: Right to pass; respect others' ideas.
- Respectful Speech: Is it true? Is it necessary? Allow time for others.
- Mindful Listening: Remember, two ears, two eyes, one mouth.
- Choose a "yes-and" attitude.
- Make each other look good.
- Confidentiality: No room for gossip.

Preparation
- Do loving kindness practice to prepare for Family Circle.
- Plan for no more than five to forty-five minutes, have a snack, or meal (less time is better in the beginning to ensure it is a positive experience). Let people know in advance about the Mindful Family Circle. Accept whoever shows up. If someone is missing, you can even set an empty chair to hold their space for another time.
- You will need a notepad and marker, a talking stick, and a light-weight ball.

Story Circle
- Bring family members together in a circle.
- State Agenda and Guidelines: "Thank you for coming. We are

having a Family Circle to tell a few family stories. The Family Circle will last thirty minutes and we will play some games, tell stories, and share food. These are the guidelines for the group (have them written out and state each one). Does anyone have any questions about the guidelines or would anyone like to add anything else?" (If anyone wants to add anything, you can write down on the guidelines paper.)

Keep things positive for the Family Circle. If things become negative, the worst thing that happens is that you end the Family Circle stating you will try again another time. The goal with Family Circle in the beginning is to share positive time together even if it's only five minutes.

Games (play two or three games per circle)
- Make Each Other Look Good Ball toss game. Count the number of passes the ball stays in the air. When you pass to another person set them up for success. Say only positive comments.
- One Word Story Game
- Made a Mistake Performance
- Rocking Practice
- Yes-And Game with planning a family picnic
- Give-and-Take Game
- What's Missing Game

Storytelling Talking Circle: First and Second Rounds
- *Opening Ritual.* Light a candle and set an intention: "My intention is to bring the family together to share family stories and have a nice experience."
- *Introduce a Talking Stick.* "Whoever holds the talking stick can talk, while the others practice good listening and wait for

their turn. We will pass the talking stick around in a clockwise direction. You also have a right to pass. We only have a short time for this so make your stories short enough that everyone gets a chance to talk. Please only share stories that make family members look good or they would be happy with you sharing."

- *First Round.* Tell a family story about an ancestor or relative that reflects a family value, like having fun or courage. Use the talking stick and tell your story first. Only the person holding the stick can talk.
- *Second Round.* Go around a second time using the prompt, "Something I take away from this is . . ." Each member goes around and states one sentence of a theme or something they take away from the stories they heard. They start with, "Something I take away from this is . . ."
- Blow out the candle.

Share Food

Sharing a special snack or a meal together is a nice way to close an activity. Family members can rotate on who chooses and brings the snacks. You can assign different items of the meal to different people.

Closing Ritual

Honor Circle. Go around in a circle and say a short compliment or nice words honoring the person on your left, until everyone around the circle has given and received a compliment.

. . .

Congratulations, you have completed Stage 2 of the mindful family journey: you have made your Mindful Family Circle.

CHAPTER 4

FAMILY JOY

Let no one ever come to you without leaving better and happier.

—Mother Teresa

I grew up in an urban environment in Southern California. The only nature close by was the grass on the front lawn and the trees. One of the things that brought me the most joy was the tree in my next-door neighbors' yard. To this day I do not know what kind of tree it was, I just know that it was the best climbing tree ever.

If you were looking at it from a bird's-eye view, you would see substantial branches that got thicker the further down they went, spiraling out like a staircase. The thickest branch was low enough for me to reach my arms around, hoist my leg over, and flip onto. From there it was possible to walk up the branches.

I would climb to the highest branch that could hold my weight and sit near what I liked to call "the bat pole," a branch that went straight up and down, and was so smooth that I could slide down to the branch below. When I was up in that tree, I was climbing, but I was also imagining entire worlds—I was shipwrecked and the tree was my home, and from there all kinds of scenarios and characters arose.

In the eighties, I ventured out into the world for an out-of-the-tree exchange student adventure. At seventeen, I went on my own to a small town in Sweden called Ulvsby where I went from living in a large, urbanized, concrete environment to a rural town in the middle of an enormous forest. The house where I lived was three stories tall and had its own sauna, a common feature in Swedish homes. The bottom floor basement was dedicated to music and stockpiled with Beatles albums and a freezer full of cardamom rolls. Out the front door was a dirt road that led to the main highway into Karlstad (an actual town); all other paths were forest.

My host family had no qualms about me wandering out alone into the wilderness, even in October, which was moose hunting season. My experience consisted of walking in the quiet, past the tall trees and shrubs, listening, watching, and wondering when I would come across a moose and suddenly being gripped by terror that something or someone was after me. Heart thumping, I would run as fast as I could back to the house, tearing through the trees and onto the gravel driveway where my younger host brother, Eric, would laugh and try to scare me even more. That brought him joy. My host father would assure me that there was nothing to be afraid of in that forest. I still get scared walking alone through the forest, but I find joy in it anyway.

Nature-based play offers children the experience of joy and awe that only a true connection with the natural world can provide. Yet, children today have fewer opportunities to play in nature, leaving them without a connection to the natural world, which is the predominant place where they develop their instincts, enliven their creativity, and experience joy. I wouldn't trade the experience in the forest or my childhood tree for any toy or game, digital or otherwise.

The tree of my childhood worked my body and it also worked my imagination. I have learned many things from nature, and especially from my relationship with that tree, including how to be present and at the same time let go enough to allow myself to experience receptive imagination. Earlier I quoted Einstein: "Imagination is more important than knowledge. For knowledge is limited to all we now know and understand, while imagination embraces the entire world, and all there ever will be to know and understand." Remember back in chapter 1 when I said we need imagination to get off the train and make a mindful life? I'm talking about receptive imagination where we create space in our minds and bodies and allow things to instinctively bubble up. I'm talking about imagination that comes from our instincts.

Awakening Instincts Practice: Beginner's Mind

In this chapter, you are going to invite your instincts to awaken to joy by being present to the natural world with something called "beginner's mind," which means seeing things as if you have never seen them before.

When my daughter was one, she tasted candy for the first time. It was Halloween night, and we were in New England because my husband was working as a Smithsonian scholar studying ancient Cahuilla artifacts related to the traditional bird songs of his tribe. We found a classic New England neighborhood, the kind with large trees and big porches covered with pumpkins and hay, to go trick-or-treating.

My daughter did not want to approach the front door of a stranger, so I went first. She wouldn't even take the candy, so I put out my hand. When I plopped the candy into her pumpkin bag, she looked down with curiosity. We proceeded to the next house, but she wasn't keeping up. When I turned to beckon her to come with me, she was walking in slow motion. She had taken the candy out of the pumpkin, unwrapped it, and popped it into her mouth. Slowly chewing, her head was cocked to the side. Every bit of her attention was focused on the novel experience of this small piece of sugar. She was in the space of beginner's mind.

To practice beginner's mind, you are going to work with a playful practice of Mindful Seeing adapted from the Wilderness Awareness School in Washington state.

MINDFUL SEEING IN NATURE

With a blank piece of paper, or your journal, and a pencil, start by going outside and opening up your senses. Listen to the sounds around you. Feel the breeze or the sun on your skin. Take a deep breath in and smell your surroundings—stay with that for five breaths, focusing your attention on the air entering and exiting your nostrils.

Drop in the question, "What brings me joy?" With your vision, look around as if you were seeing things for the first time. Try to let go of preconceived notions of what things are. Notice colors, shapes, lines. Notice things in front of you, to the sides of you, above you, below you, even behind you. Drop in the question again, "What brings me joy?"

Walk around, as best as you can, being guided by your instincts, and stop in front of something that gives you joy (even if it's just a drop of something that could bring a small smile to your lips). Once you have found this joy-inducing entity, really look at it, again, as if you were seeing it for the first time.

After you have taken it in, turn your back to it and don't look at it again. Close your eyes and get the image firmly in your mind. Without looking back, open your eyes, and draw the object. When you are finished, turn back to the object and notice what you captured and what you missed. Really take the image in a second time.

After you have taken it in, turn your back to it again and don't look at it. Close your eyes and get the image firmly in your mind. Without looking back, open your eyes, and fill in more of the object that you originally missed. When you are finished, turn back to the object and notice what you captured and what you missed. Repeat this one final time.

Put this drawing in a place where you can see it on a regular basis.

This can also be done as a family activity, with family members meeting back afterward to share their experiences and their drawings.

Why Play Matters for Joy

Play is vitally important for both adults and children as it cultivates joy, builds and strengthens relationships, waters the seeds of respect, and promotes healthy brain development linked to executive skill functioning (regulating emotions, planning, and problem-solving) and creativity. Neuroscientist Jaak Panksepp from Washington State University writes that play builds pro-social brains so humans know how to interact with each other in positive ways. The experience of play literally changes brain connections in our prefrontal cortex, which is related to executive functioning (Hamilton 2014). To produce this kind of impact from play, children need to engage in play that is free with no coaches or rulebooks—imaginative play.

I have a friend who is prone to depression. She is a hardworking researcher who puts in tireless hours. She told me once that she has to force herself to stop working at a certain time each day or her depression grows. She has to find time for play. I think of her when I see my daughter up late studying. She's focused and concentrated, she gets good grades, but I worry when there's more tiredness than joy in her face. I have to remember to help her play; and even harder, I have to remember to stop my work and embody the spirit of play and joy in myself.

In the first three chapters you have worked on awakening your instincts and stopping, noticing, and offering kindness. You have completed the first two stages of this guidebook: Crafting a Family North Star Intention and Family Circle, which set up the conditions for the Spirit of Respect to be present in a mindful family ensemble. These two stages are foundational for what comes next. They provide the space to transmit the values you envisioned in the Family North Star Intention.

Starting with the foundational value of cultivating joy, you are going to use the skills you have learned up to this point to weave joy into the fabric of your family life. The two tasks for this month's mission are 1) Joyful Moments Practice (a form of offering kindness to your child), which will be done one-on-one with your child (regardless of age); and 2) Joy Planning, with improv games focused on collaboration, team building, and brainstorming, which you will practice in Family Circle.

JOYFUL MOMENTS

Joyful Moments practice uses the skills learned in the Finding the Treasure practice, now with a focus on joy. This practice can be done both informally and formally. Informal Joyful Moments practice centers around noticing when joy is present in a family member or about to rear its beautiful head through smiles, laughter, enthusiasm, or awe and giving it the focus of your attention to help it grow and expand, truly savoring the moment. Formal Joyful Moments practice involves burying (planting) the treasure, treasure hunting, and savoring the treasure.

Joyful Moments

Finding Joy	Mindfulness Practice	Tasks
Burying (planting) the Treasure	*Appreciative joy practice*	*Joyful presence* *Set up the space* *Screen out distractions* *Choose the activity*
Treasure Hunting	*Child as a Mindfulness Bell (Stop and Notice)* *Beginner's mind* *Finding the treasure by offering kindness in the form of joy*	*Intention setting: cultivate joy with a curious, enthusiastic, genuine, "yes-and" attitude* *Naming (positive emotions and behavior)* *Playful connection: suggesting, joining, or appreciative audience*
Savoring the Treasure	*Observing and listening*	*Savoring and expanding*

1. Burying (Planting) the Treasure

Burying the Treasure is about preparation: setting up conditions so joy is more likely to emerge. This involves four steps, which include appreciative joy; setting up the space for the conditions of connection, respect, and joy to grow; screening out distractions; and choosing activities that elicit joyful moments. Burying the Treasure also involves a formal Appreciative Joy practice in order to cultivate a joyful presence.

Formal Practice: Stopping, Noticing, and Offering Kindness— Appreciative Joy

Bringing a joyful presence is one way of offering kindness to your family members. A joyful presence includes recognizing joy in yourself, appreciating joy in others, and setting an intention to have a joyful attitude that includes manifesting enthusiasm, curiosity, genuineness, and a "yes-and" position. Appreciative Joy is a formal way of cultivating a joyful presence, which you can do in preparation for Joyful Moments practice.

APPRECIATIVE JOY FOR YOUR CHILD

Begin by sitting comfortably on a chair or the floor. Notice the feel of your feet touching the ground, your body connecting with the chair or ground underneath you. Take a few deep breaths and then let your breath return to its natural rhythm, whatever it is: shallow, deep, fast, slow. Notice if it changes as you pay attention to it. Breathe into your belly, chest, or nose (anchoring your breath to that part of your body), following the breath all the way in and all the way out. Notice when the mind wanders and gently, kindly bring it back to the breath.

After five minutes of breath practice, bring to mind an image of something that has brought you joy, or that you imagine could bring you joy. Imagine or feel that person, event, or thing in front of you. Notice where the feeling shows up in your body. How do you know you're feeling joy? If it's difficult to access, what do you imagine it would feel like? What did you love to do as a child?

Stay focused on sensations, as opposed to thoughts. If thoughts are present, notice them and bring your attention back to the sensations of joy in your body. With this energy, or imagined energy, picture your child and say the following phrases. Let whatever arises, arise. Don't try to change it, just notice it with an open curiosity.

May your peace and joy expand, forever and ever.
I am happy for you.

Repeat.

Then direct these phrases toward yourself:

May my peace and joy expand, forever and ever.
May I be happy.

Repeat.

If it's difficult to experience joy, that's okay; what's important is that the seeds of joy are planted. One thing that can help bring the quality of enthusiasm is a smile. Research shows that smiling releases oxytocin, a feel-good hormone—even a forced smile works (Spector 2017). We will focus on the qualities of curiosity, genuineness, and a "yes-and" attitude in the treasure hunting section.

Setting Up the Space

The optimal space for formal Joyful Moments with your child is an environment where rules and adult-imposed boundaries are minimized, so that your child is free to safely explore, create, and be seen. For example, if you are doing a Joyful Moments activity with paint, it is best not done on carpet. If the space is outside, the boundaries of where not to go (due to safety issues) is important to establish beforehand.

Screening Out Distractions

Creating a distraction-free zone where outside forces like ring tones, screen time, or other family members won't pull the attention away from your child is critical for creating a present moment focus where receptive imagination can arise and you can notice the emerging joy. This practice can be a relaxing break from the multitasking of family life. In addition to external distractions, we also have internal ones. Because we are so used to being overstimulated with media, multi-tasking, and interruptions, boredom or restlessness may arise with this present moment focus. If this happens, allow it to be there. Notice how it shows up in your body in terms of sensations and then direct your behavior back to your child. In Joyful Moments, allow whatever is there to be there, turning up the corners of your mouth and staying present in this moment with your child, even if all you feel is a drop of joyful presence.

Choosing the Activity

Choosing the activity can come from you or your child, but it should be an activity that has the capacity for joy to emerge. Be sure to also include activities for receptive imagination. For example, a board game your child enjoys can provide moments for joy to emerge but is limited in opportunities for receptive imagination. Painting, make believe play, building a fort, or creating a new recipe are opportunities for receptive imagination. Once the activity is chosen, gather the necessary materials. It is important to consider your child's temperament in choosing the activity and materials you are using. For example, a walk or a ball toss for a child that doesn't talk much can set the stage for necessary communication, creative expression, and joy to emerge. The age of your child will also dictate the types of activities and materials you choose.

2. Treasure Hunting for Joyful Moments

Now it's time for Treasure Hunting for Joyful Moments. You can do this informally anytime by stopping, noticing, and bringing a joyful presence to what your child is already doing. You will also practice this formally with one-on-one Joyful Moments dates with your child. Prepare for this with an Appreciative Joy practice. Treasure Hunting for Joyful Moments combines several mindfulness practices including Child as a Mindfulness Bell, beginner's mind, and Finding the Treasure. The tasks include Intention Setting, Naming, and Playful Connection through making suggestions, joining, or being an appreciative audience. Being present with your children is a present to them, and it is powerful medicine. In the last chapter, we talked about six hours of magic as being protective in terms of spending time together as a family. Bringing your presence to the process is like an essential oil; it's the essence of the practice and it builds the Spirit of Respect. This practice can be as little as ten minutes a day with your child or you might like to spend several hours. What's important is consistency of practice; keep bringing your attention to how you interact with your child.

Intention Setting

The intention you set for Joyful Moments practice is to connect with your child by bringing a joyful presence, which includes an attitude of enthusiasm, curiosity, genuineness, and "yes-and" attitude.

Beginner's Mind

For your Joyful Moments practice, start with Child as a Mindfulness Bell, stopping and noticing your child, with beginner's mind. Be curious. We often see what confirms our biases. Our brains work in a way that once we think we have enough information, we stop processing and fill in the gaps with our ideas of things. Instead of seeing the child in front of us right now, we see an idea we have of the child, a preconceived notion. Try to erase what you know about your child and see who they have grown into in this moment. Remember how much you missed in the Mindful Seeing in nature practice? How much do you miss seeing in your child? Look at them with beginner's mind, as if you have never seen them before, like you looked at them when they were first born.

Naming Emotions and Behavior

Naming involves focusing the spotlight of your attention on your child and narrating the story (positive emotions and behaviors) of what is unfolding in the moment with curiosity, enthusiasm, genuineness, and a "yes-and" attitude. In this story, your child is the director of the play and the main star. Name your own positive emotions, as well as your child's positive emotions and behaviors with an eye toward joy. The underlying message you give to your child with naming is, "I see you. I am here with you. I value you. You delight me." You are hunting for the joy in the moments and naming is your shovel.

At first your children may look at you strangely, but soon they will enjoy it. They know they have your presence and the experience of being in the lead is something rare for children in this world. If you find your child acting aggressively or going beyond the initial boundaries set, turn your spotlight of attention on your own breathing. If this doesn't help change the tone of the interaction, you can also end the time for the day and return to it later. This time should never be punitive; always leave the door open for a fresh start at another time. We all have bad days and unskillful behavior patterns are difficult to correct. With persistence, kindness, and a Family North Star Intention focus, these patterns change.

Connecting: Suggesting, Joining, or Being an Appreciative Audience

When initiating playful connection with your child you have three choices: offering a suggestion, joining what they are doing, or being an appreciative audience.

Suggesting. Suggest an activity that has a high likelihood for joyful moments to emerge. Take into consideration what your child likes as well as their temperament. This can involve structured as well as unstructured activities, but be sure to include some unstructured activities in nature, which allow for receptive imagination and nature connections to emerge. Examples of activities are in the table below.

Joyful Things to Do

Structured Activities	Unstructured Activities
Board games	Playing with Legos
Tag	Building something (a fort, a birdhouse)
Hide and seek	Making a new recipe (try making a smoothie)
Video games	Painting, drawing, coloring
Sport play (tennis, soccer, baseball, basketball) not focused on winning	Ball toss (following their lead in conversation)
Amusement park rides	Hiking, walking

Joining. In joining an activity, you notice something your child is already doing. You watch and ask to join in or slowly start naming and mirroring the activity ("I like how you are doing that, I want to do that too") and emotions ("You look like you are having fun. I feel happy watching you. I want to do that with you"), maintaining a "yes-and" attitude ("Yes, you can leave out the banana for the smoothie, and the extra strawberries you are adding look delicious," "Yes, you are building a spaceship to the moon, and I bet it can fly across the entire galaxy"). The important thing is to maintain a joyful presence, following your child's lead.

Appreciative Audience. Being an appreciative audience requires good observation and listening skills. This brings in the skill of Mindful listening that we established with the Family Circle. You continually bring your attention back to your breath in your body, knowing you are here in this present moment, letting go of preconceived notions of who your child is and even what this activity together is supposed to be. Shine your spotlight of attention on your child with a joyful presence. This can be done with more than one child, but it's more challenging to divide your spotlight among multiple children. Having individual attention is important, so be sure to give small doses of one-on-one Joyful Moments daily when starting out.

TIME FOR JOYFUL MOMENTS

With Joyful Moments Time, you set the stage so few rules need to be imposed on the activity. If there are rules that need to be established, let the child know up front but keep them to a minimum. Gather whatever materials are necessary and limit distractions.

Once this is established (or if your child has already set the stage and you notice them engaged in an activity), shine your attention on your child with a curious, enthusiastic, genuine attitude, watching for joy to manifest. Name positive emotions in yourself and your child, as well as using descriptive words for what they are doing. ("You are singing a song. Your singing makes me feel happy.")

Make suggestions for joy-inducing activities, join the play with a "yes-and" attitude and Mirroring (always keeping the spotlight on your child), or be an appreciative audience using your observation and listening skills.

When joy does emerge, savor and expand it through focused attention. If play becomes aggressive or goes beyond established boundaries, return the spotlight of attention to your own breathing. If the disruption continues, calmly stop and resume on another day. This is not a time for correction or punishment.

When you name, make suggestions, or join, do so with an eye toward things that are playful, fun, and could spark joy (i.e., Suggesting: "Let's sing a song together, singing with you makes my heart feel happy." Joining: "You are making a strawberry smoothie, yum! I want to make one just like you."). Examples of Joyful Moments and activities with different age groups are included below as suggestions.

Toddlers

Activity: Hands-on toys and make believe activities work well for this age group. Example: Playing with big Legos.

Naming: Naming with this age group is very descriptive. Find things to name that genuinely spark your child's curiosity and enthusiasm. Let your child be in the lead most of the time, responding to their verbalizations and behavior with a "yes-and" attitude.

Suggestion: "Let's build an amusement park with the Legos. That would be so much fun."

Joining: "Yes-And" Attitude and Mirroring. The parent notices their child is playing with Legos. "I feel happy when I watch you building with the Legos. You are putting a blue Lego on top of a red Lego. One, two, three Legos. I want to build something just like you." To mirror in the activity the parent can build the same thing the child is building, pacing slightly behind the child and continuing with naming, "I like what you are building. You look happy. I want to build one just like you. That would make me happy. It's so nice of you to share the Legos with me."

Appreciative Audience: "I like how you are playing gently with the toys. It's so nice of you to include me in your play by letting me watch, that makes me feel very happy."

School-Aged children

Activity: More sophisticated hands-on toys. Coloring, painting, and make believe activities work well with this age group. Example: Painting.

Naming: Naming with this age group is descriptive.

Suggestion: "Let's paint together. That would be so much fun."

Joining: "Yes-And" Attitude and Mirroring. The parent notices their child is painting.

Example of making the naming playful: "The maiden's paintings became so popular that an apprentice came to study under her. The apprentice liked to work with the maiden because she was kind, she shared her paints, and she always gave compliments." To mirror in the activity the parent can build the same thing the child is building, pacing slightly behind the child and continuing with naming, "I want to make a picture just like you." "It's so nice to paint together."

Appreciative Audience: Example of making naming playful: "Once there was a young maiden who was painting a beautiful picture. She used lovely colors in her picture. It relaxes me to sit here and watch you paint. I feel happy. Thank you for letting me watch." (Child dips the paintbrush in another color, but it mixes with the first and doesn't come out like they want it to on the paper. They dip their brush in the water.) "The maiden wanted a different color, so she cleaned her brush and tried again. This particular maiden always stuck with things, even when they were hard. She was such a good problem solver that the other villagers in the kingdom learned from her, and their lives were better because of it."

Teenagers

Activity: Craft projects, cooking with recipes they create themselves, walks in nature, conversations on topics they find interesting—use your mindful listening skills.

Naming: Naming with this age group is more reflective and paraphrasing of the direct activity or conversation topic. Listen for the emotion underneath the message.

Suggestion: Say your teen comments that they are stressed about finals coming up and frustrated by their math teacher. You can say,: "I'm glad you're taking some time to relax before hitting the books. I know there's a lot of pressure on you right now. It doesn't help having a teacher that isn't explaining the concepts clearly. You must be really frustrated." (Note: This isn't a time to solve the problem, just reflect the situation and underlying emotion with empathy.) "I remember a teacher like that when I was in college. I even went to ask for help and their explanations confused me more. I ended up going to the library and teaching myself from books. Would you like to play a game of King's Crown to de-stress?"

Joining: "You're making a smoothie. That sounds delicious. I want to try your recipe. Can I make one too? How about I get some fancy cups to put it in?"

Appreciative Audience: Teen is building a model airplane: "I'm excited to see how the airplane is coming along. Some of those pieces are so small. I'm impressed at how well you manipulate them. You really have a lot of patience and that makes the wing turn out like the real deal. It's nice to watch you work."

3. Savoring the Treasure

Once the treasure of a joyful moment is found, it is important to give it the focus of your attention. What you pay attention to often expands, and that is what you are trying to do—grow the treasure. With present moment focus on the joy (a smile, a laugh, interest, awe) as it emerges, you can expand the moment, as well as register it within your emotional memory. Researcher and author Barbara Fredrickson's Broaden-and-Build Theory of Positive Emotions states that positive emotions promote discovery of novel and creative actions, ideas, and social bonds, which in turn build that individual's personal resources, ranging from physical and intellectual resources, to social and psycho-logical resources. It takes ten to fifteen seconds of focus for the emotion to get into our emotional memory, which can work like a daily vitamin for our health and well-being.

One morning, I got up early to let my dog out. As he bounded to the door, I smiled, witnessing his enthusiasm. I decided to build on the joy. I smiled and clapped my hands. This increased his joy and he ran around the house at top speed, coming to a screeching halt just before I thought he was going to mow me down. I did a circle dance by turning in a circle enthusiastically and clapping, and then he started to do the dance with me. As long as I stayed present and enthusiastic, my dog kept running and doing the circle dance. I was able to savor and broaden the joyful moment. It's the same with our children. (And all our family members.) We need to savor the joyful moments with the people we love, allowing them to linger and registering them within our emotional memories.

Joy Planning

For Joy Planning, this month you are going to plan a fun family activity during Mindful Family Circle, working together as a family ensemble focused on joy. Improv tools you will use include the Mirror Game (listening and observation skills), Pass the Focus Game (collaboration and team-building skills), and Gifting (Offering Kindness).

You will engage in a brainstorming activity to plan family fun, further enhancing creativity and promoting feelings of indispensability for all members.

Brainstorming

Brainstorming can be used to generate a list of ideas and solve problems, which can lead to heightened creativity and skills to assist in thinking outside of the box. With brainstorming a facilitator sets up a structure and lays out parameters in which members are encouraged to come up with as many ideas as possible and all ideas are encouraged. Criticizing is avoided and a "yes-and" attitude is promoted. This opens up space for more creativity and provides a format in which everyone contributes.

Creative Brainstorming Steps

1) Assigning Roles. It may be good to start this after people are familiar with Family Circle. Roles include Facilitator, Note Taker, Space Setter, and Food Preparer. You can assign additional roles as necessary so everyone feels indispensable or rotate roles. For the first few meetings it is important that you are the facilitator to set the foundation for a healthy brainstorming process. In fact, initially you may want to play all the roles to teach the format and process.

2) Setting Up the Space. Set up a circular space with no barriers. Place the talking stick or talking pieces in the middle. Getting rid of barriers encourages everyone to be present and participate. Large paper or a pad of paper is necessary for the brainstorming session. Each member will also need their own paper and pen to write their individual ideas.

3) Preparing Food. This family member prepares the snacks for the activity. They should be simple snacks that are easy to eat so energy can be directed to the brainstorming activity. Having the food at the end of the brainstorming session is recommended, but it could be passed out during group brainstorming.

4) Setting the Intention. As part of the opening ritual, light a candle and set an intention for the meeting. The facilitator models this by setting an intention for the circle, perhaps related to your theme, for example, "This circle is dedicated to fun and joy in our family." The intention is to bring a Joyful Presence with an enthusiastic, curious, genuine, "yes-and" attitude to plan family fun. Each member can then come forward and make their own intention. Everyone does not need to do this. If multiple people are going to make intentions, it is good to have a bell they can ring or multiple candles they can light as they come forward to signify their intention. They can either make a silent or verbal intention. Once intentions are set, the facilitator reviews the Spirit of Respect Guidelines and states the agenda. For this first brainstorming Family Circle a set agenda is included at the end of this chapter.

5) *Engage with a Fun Activity.* Family Circle always includes a fun activity. For this circle, Mirroring and Pass the Focus games are played.

MIRRORING GAME

Mirroring requires observation and listening skills. This game can be powerful for the one being mirrored to feel seen, and promotes healthy self-esteem, respect, and connection. A parent can practice this with another family member one on one, or even with the television, turning down the sound and mirroring what is observed. For Family Circle, split into pairs. If your family is not made up of an even number of people, have one person be an observer and change roles so everyone gets a turn in both positions, of mirroring and being mirrored.

The Mirror: In pairs, the person who is being mirrored initiates small facial and body movements. The other person, who is mirroring, copies the person's movements as if they were a mirror. Then they switch roles. The mirrorer becomes the mirrored, and the mirrored becomes the mirrorer. Finally, the pair do this activity with no one assigned to lead and see if they naturally switch back and forth from leading to following.

PASS THE FOCUS GAME

The Pass the Focus game is a give-and-take activity in which everyone contributes. Some people more naturally gravitate to leadership roles and others to follower roles. This activity helps give everyone practice in both. Knowing how to play both roles is important in the family and as a life skill in the larger world. Wharton's top-rated psychology professor and author Adam Grant's research on give and take found that givers are more productive than takers in the field of engineering. In his research, the highest achievers were most driven to help others.

Pass the Focus: Members pass the focus around the room by one person making eye contact with a member. Once that happens, the member accepts. Others then try to take the focus back by blocking the focus or getting the person's attention in some other manner.

Practice going back and forth in giving and taking focus. Give focus by looking at someone or touching their shoulder, players can mirror them as well in mannerisms or verbalizations. Then they take the focus back, and the other person gives the focus to them. Players can give focus to anyone, and partners can do this process back and forth.

The facilitator can call switch and new pairs are formed. This can easily break into chaos, but either way it's a place to work from and develop give-and-take skills.

6) Topic Setting. Review the Spirit of Respect Guidelines and the topic and format for the brainstorming session.

Brainstorming Session

1) Set the Topic. Planning Family Fun.

2) *Imagination Generation.* The facilitator has the space setter pass out paper and pens and instructs everyone to write down as many ideas as possible in five minutes, reminding them that the idea is to come up with as many ideas as possible no matter how crazy they seem. The "no matter how crazy" guideline is important because it opens up brain flexibility and creates an atmosphere of fun.

To harness the benefits of both the group and individual brainstorming, first have members write down their ideas on paper and then share with the larger group using a talking stick process, which is followed by a second round of brainstorming. We start with individual brainstorming because there is some research to suggest that individual brainstorming can lead to more creative ideas than group brainstorming as individuals can be more influenced by the group and come up with less ideas. The key to creative brainstorming is coming up with as many ideas as possible, no matter how crazy.

3) *Idea Sharing.* Once ideas are generated, people share their ideas in clockwise order with a talking stick. Anyone can start. If a member chooses not to share, they simply take the stick and pass it to their left. Once all ideas are out, the group opens up the discussion where members share any additional ideas in a group format. This can be facilitated with a talking piece set in the middle of the circle that members pick up and return as they are ready to share. After that, members pick their top two or three ideas and they are recorded and discussed until one idea or a combination is chosen.

4) *Finalizing the Plan.* The plan is recorded on paper by the note taker and details such as when, where, who, what, and how are listed.

5) *Review of Activity.* This activity can be reviewed at the next Family Circle.

6) *Closing.* This discussion closes by ritual. Play the Gifting Game and blow out the candle.

GIFTING GAME

Gifting helps generate feelings of generosity and good will in the context of play. This activity helps realign habits of opposing people and helps to foster habits of supporting and building on each other's ideas to further spur creativity.

Gifting: Divide into groups of two. One person is the giver and the other is the receiver. The giver brings an imaginary present that they know the receiver would love to have. The receiver accepts the present with gratitude and makes comments about the gift. In the end the receiver is the one who names what they receive, with the giver trying to guess from the receiver's comments. Switch places and repeat so everyone has a chance in both roles.

Members can then share a meal or snack together, unless this was already done during the brainstorming session.

...

Congratulations, you have completed Stage 3 of the mindful family journey: Cultivating Family Joy.

CHAPTER 5

MINDFUL FAMILY MEALS

One of the very nicest things about life is the way
we must regularly stop whatever it is that we are
doing and devote our attention to eating.

—Luciano Pavarotti

Sharing mindful family meals is a practice of reclaiming sovereignty in our lives through listening to our body's wisdom and freeing ourselves from following the unhealthy dictates of artificial society regarding the food we eat. It is a practice that we can use to strengthen our intuitive way of knowing, improve our health, strengthen family bonds, and transmit mindful family values.

With artificial society comes artificial food that is literally killing us. The standard American diet, with processed foods high in sugar, salt, and fat made from genetically modified ingredients laden with pesticides is vastly different from the foods that sustained people for thousands of years. Dr. David Katz from Yale University's Prevention Research Center states that a diet of minimally processed food, predominantly plants, is associated with health promotion and disease prevention; yet in 2015, the *American Journal of Clinical Nutrition* reported that 61 percent of the foods that Americans buy are highly processed (Poti et. al). As a result, our society has high rates of health problems like heart disease, stroke, and diabetes, even among children.

Chocolate is the food that bears ancient wisdom. Chocolate is often linked with the Swiss, but it is actually an indigenous food from this continent. It comes from a bean that was cultivated by the Olmec Indians and later the Mayans. It was so revered that Cortez became aware of this delicacy through a chocolate honoring celebration he witnessed among the Indigenous people of Mesoamerica.

After he experienced chocolate in the form of a drink, he took it back to Spain where it became a drink reserved for royalty. It was laborious to make, so the Spanish developed a slave trade to cultivate the cocoa bean and make it profitable. Eventually, the Swiss took it and added milk and other ingredients. When it became available to the masses, it was cut with other ingredients until it stopped being primarily chocolate and became another processed food.

Recently, studies have found that real chocolate may lower cholesterol and reduce the risk of cardiovascular disease. You'll be happy to know that scientists at Harvard Medical School report that drinking two cups of hot chocolate a day may keep the brain healthy and prevent memory decline in older people. But only if it's chocolate that is similar to its original form, which is impossible to find in our modern world.

Today, dark chocolate is the closest we get to the original Olmec chocolate. As chocolate was modified further and further from its original form, it was developed into something we still call chocolate, but this artificial or processed chocolate lost many of its health benefits. Rather than being a food that helps, now it is a food that puts our bodies at risk. Many types of chocolate on the market today are processed, containing minimal to no real chocolate and instead they have ingredients like refined sugar and fats that are bad for you. Sound familiar?

To get the best health benefits, it is necessary to go back to chocolate closer to its traditional form. Knowing what chocolate is helps us to find actual chocolate. Similarly, knowing who we really are and where we come from helps us to live our lives from an internal compass that is much healthier than what we are fed from colonized society.

In this chapter, your mission is to begin reclaiming sovereignty over the food you eat through five eating principles, which are tied to the three Mindful Family Values.

MINDFUL EATING PRINCIPLES

Ancestral strength and knowledge

- Look deeply into the history of your food.
- Incorporate ancestral foods and stories into mealtimes.
- Shift from external to internal markers for what you eat, why you eat, and the effect it has on your body and mind.

Spirit of respect

- Create a mealtime environment to build family bonds and transmit family values.

Cultivate joy

- Savor and enjoy your mealtime experiences.

Value 1 | Ancestral Strength and Knowledge

MINDFUL EATING PRINCIPLE #1

Look Deeply into the History of Your Food

Understanding where what you are eating comes from is an important practice of mindful eating. I was at a dinner party recently where a woman from Singapore told me that there is a Chinese saying, "Know where every sip of water comes from."

When frozen TV dinners first became available, they seemed like a great idea. I remember eating Stouffers on a TV tray in front of the television as a special treat. Each food had its own special section in the aluminum platter. Who knew that processed food was part of what would lead to a diabetes epidemic, taking us further away from what is best for our bodies? Strawberries used to be sweet and tomatoes were a delicacy. Now, good tasting fruit without pesticides is hard to find.

Modern societal systems have limited our food choices from the types of grains available to us to the number of products we can have that aren't genetically engineered. If food was already good and healthy, then why did we get rid of it and choose things that are killing us? Why are we limited on the types of grain produced in the world today? Why don't we have real chocolate anymore, like the Olmecs did?

Let's try a History of Food practice to develop awareness about what we are putting into our bodies. I recommend a raisin, but you can try this with any type of food. Hold the piece of food in your hand while you read the following passage.

HISTORY OF FOOD PRACTICE

With a raisin in front of you, close your eyes and take a few natural breaths, following the in-breath and out-breath fully.

Place the raisin in your palm and contemplate its history. Where did this raisin come from? What was involved in getting this raisin to where it is in your palm now?

The sun, the rain, and soil nurtured its growth into a grape, which someone or many people planted, and harvested: the people who picked the grapes, the transporters who delivered it to the factory where it would be made into a raisin. Even the people who made the trucks that transported the raisin were involved in getting this here.

Then there were the people who packaged the raisins, the store that shelved them, and the person who purchased them. Until this one little raisin finally got to you.

That's one way of looking at the history of where your food comes from. Imagine all the natural processes and people involved in bringing this to you, the vast interconnectedness and web of life that supports you and grows your food.

This raisin is sunlight converted to food. When you eat the raisin, know that you are eating a piece of the sun.

MINDFUL EATING PRINCIPLE #2

Incorporate Ancestral Foods and Stories into Mealtimes

To further your ancestral strength and knowledge, introduce food from your heritage in their traditional forms. Include recipes from your culture and the stories of how these foods and recipes made their way into your family. This can instill in your children a sense of pride in who they are and where they come from, and if it is passed down, a connection to the relative who is the knowledge carrier of this recipe.

When I was growing up, we lived with my grandmother from the South; she made dinner every night. After school, I played outside with the other children and she would call me in when dinner was ready. We would sit around the table and eat fried chicken, some vegetable like green beans, bread and butter, and sometimes mashed potatoes and gravy. I learned the value of family meals by watching my grandmother's behavior. I learned what she valued by seeing her ensure that dinner was on the table each night, and that was after getting up at 3:30 or 4:00 a.m. and working all day. She taught us that eating this family meal together was important.

The Cahuilla Indians of Southern California used the acorns from oak trees to make a staple dish called *weewish*. It constituted 65 percent of their diet. It was healthy for the heart and preventative of diabetes, which is a huge health problem in our communities today. Learn what the Indigenous people where you live ate. Think about where you could get real food, locally grown, in its natural state.

MINDFUL EATING PRINCIPLE #3

Shift from External to Internal Cues about What You Eat, Why You Eat, and the Effect It Has on Your Body and Mind

We eat primarily from external cues. How much food is on our plate, food pictures, food smells, food facts, and eating times are all external sources telling us when and what to eat. Everyday our attention is captured by food images. Food information gathered from digital sources influences 70 percent of the food choices we make according to the *Journal of American Dietetic Association* (Wasinek 2006). The way food looks on a plate can even impact how we perceive the flavor and how much of it we eat. Make this knowledge work for you. Repeated visual exposure of vegetables through a children's picture book increases liking of vegetables (Houston-Price et al. 2006, *Journal of Experimental Child Psychology)*.

Have you ever noticed that when you are hungry, your sense of smell actually improves? Our sense of smell is processed at a lower level of consciousness than other sensory experiences. The olfactory bulb, which processes smells, is located in the brain's limbic area. This part of the brain is also responsible for processing emotions and memories. When I first listed my home for rent, I read that I should boil cinnamon, so when the potential renter walked in they would feel a sense of nostalgia. I did this and not only did I rent to the first visitor, but he talked about getting our children together when the rest of his family moved down. Retailers routinely use this tactic. Nike found that when it used smells to sell products, sales increased by 80 percent.

Our senses are being overstimulated so we will eat more and our internal compass is thrown off by this. Processed foods are often ultra-flavorized to increase desirability and craving. If your child has sat around eating candy and now it's time for an apple, it's probably going to seem like a bland choice. According to *Psychology Today*, in the US, 68.8 percent of the population is either obese, or overweight. Yet, we have so much external information from experts about dieting and what we should and shouldn't eat. The problem is that we rarely tune into our bodies in the present moment, while we are eating, to tap into this natural source of wisdom regarding what's healthiest for us. Strengthen your intuition and build awareness by reflecting on three questions.

1) Why am I eating?
2) What am I eating?
3) How does what I am eating make me feel?

Get educated about food, but test this information out with your own experiences of eating. Eat when you're hungry, stop when you're full, know what's in what you're eating, and eat a variety of natural foods.

Let's try a mindful eating practice to help gain awareness of what you are eating and how it impacts your body. Choose any food to do this activity. Before you start, have the food in hand. You can listen to this practice on our website or have someone read you the passage.

MINDFUL EATING PRACTICE

Before you eat the food, rate your hunger on a scale of 0 (no hunger at all) to 7 (famished, as hungry as you've ever been). Check in with your body to see if you are starving, satisfied, or full.

Then place the food in your hand. Approach this food as if you don't know anything about it and are seeing it for the first time. With just your eyes, look at this food. Notice the colors, shapes, textures that you see.

Now, bring the food to your nose and smell it. Notice the aroma and the impact that has on your body.

Next, place the food in your mouth, but don't chew it. You can press on it with your tongue. Notice what happens in your mouth, notice the feel of the food as you roll it around on your tongue.

Take one bite and notice what happens. Notice the sensations in your mouth, the taste, the texture.

Bring your attention to your stomach, and again rate your hunger on a scale of 1–7.

Continue chewing the food and swallow it. See if you can notice the food going through the digestion system, or feel the impact in your body of eating the food.

When you have finished and can no longer taste the food, do a final rating of your hunger on a scale of 0 (not hunger at all) to 7 (famished, as hungry as you've ever been).

Value 2 | Spirit of Respect

MINDFUL EATING PRINCIPLE #4

Create a Mealtime Environment to Build Family Bonds and Transmit Family Values

Family meals have their own chapter in this guidebook because family meal time gives you superpowers. Family meals may reduce disordered eating by 35 percent, increase healthy eating by 24 percent, and decrease the chance of being overweight by 12 percent (Hammons and Fiese 2011). Studies also find that family mealtimes lead to children's greater academic achievement and improved psychological well-being as well as a lesser likelihood of getting into trouble (Council of Economic Advisers, 2000; Eisenberg et al. 2004, 2009; Fulkerson et al. 2006, 2009; CASA 2010). Family meals nourish our bodies, minds, and hearts.

There is the food you eat and there is the ambiance you eat it in. Setting the family meal environment adds a power boost to the family meal and incorporates the mindful family values of respect and joy. To set the environment, we will work with consistent mealtimes, limiting distractions, including a story of the day, beautifying the area, and adding fun.

Building the Mealtime Environment

Consistency. Consistent family mealtimes help to establish a routine and reduce the hectic pace of life so members can arrive to the table with a calmer energy. In the beginning, it may feel difficult to stop the craziness of life and eat, but over time it will become a habit. Most research notes some type of improvement in child outcomes when a family participates in at least three family meals together a week. If your family life is busy, start small with one family meal a week, then move to two, slowly increasing the frequency.

I'm pretty consistent with exercising. I do some form of exercise at least five times a week, and have done so for the past twenty-five years. I'm not a person who initially loved exercise, so when I started, I needed to make a commitment to exercise at least three times a week for fifteen minutes. So, if it was eleven at night and I was in danger of not meeting my goal, I would walk around my apartment. This may not have done a lot for my heart, but setting aside the space on a consistent basis for exercise turned into a healthy lifetime habit, one that I carry with me to this day. The key to developing a habit is consistency.

Limit Distractions. Mealtimes are one of the most common times children communicate with parents, so turn off all electronic devices and other likely distractions. Pediatrician Jenny Radesky from Boston University Medical Center observed fifty-five different groups of parents eating with their children at fast food establishments. She found that forty of the fifty-five parents were more involved with their mobile phone devices than they were with their kids. Even more alarming was that with younger kids acting out increased while parents were on the phone. Many perfectly good parents get pulled in by the lure of digital devices. What's important to understand is the strength of these lures and that they have on impact on relationships with our families.

Story of the Day. Having family members share a story of the day at the dinner table can help them connect with what life away from family members has been like, provide support, or highlight what is most salient to each family member. These can be new learnings, funny things that happened, or things for which people are grateful. You can use the rose, thorn, bud game as part of this practice.

ROSE, THORN, BUD

Ask your child to observe a rose. Roses have flowers as well as thorns and rosebuds. A rose represents something you are grateful for that happened in the day; a thorn represents something that wasn't so good. A bud represents what you're hoping for tomorrow. You can then ask your child to share their day using the metaphors of the rose, thorn, and bud. Encouraging your young children to tell stories at the dinner table has the added benefit of establishing confident public speaking skills.

Beautify the Area. One of the roles family members can play is to create beauty for the meal. This can be done through setting the table, presenting food on the plate, adding a beautiful food or table item, or providing nice background music and lighting. The Navajo have a ceremony called the Beauty Way. One of the teachings is that surrounding yourself in four directions of beauty can bring up your mood and even alleviate depression.

Value 3 | Cultivating Joy

MINDFUL EATING PRINCIPLE #5
Savor and Enjoy Your Mealtime Experiences

Savoring

Taking time to savor a bite of a favorite food is a delightful experience. How many times have you eaten something you enjoy without even tasting it? This often leaves us wanting more. Savoring our food is a good practice for bringing ourselves back to the present moment and noticing with curiosity what the food tastes like, and really taking time to let that experience sink into our bodies and memory.

Take the first bite or first ten minutes of a meal together in silence, which interrupts mindless eating habits, and focus on the food visually, how it smells, and tasting it one bite at a time. Researchers from the University of Birmingham report that chewing your food fully decreases later hunger and snacking (Higgs et al. 2013). Chew the food until you no longer taste any flavor. Slowing down chewing, eating in silence, and putting utensils down between bites all help this savoring and slowing down process.

> ### TIPS FOR COOKING TOGETHER AS A JOYFUL MOMENT
> Let the child lead the process, whether it's making smoothies or sandwiches. The following tips might help you to keep encouraging your child to cook with joy:
>
> - Following the child's lead
> - Being curious and enthusiastic
> - Enjoying having beginner's mind as if you do not know how to cook and they are the expert
> - Narrating the cooking experience like a storyteller
> - Having fun and not being attached to the end result

Enjoy: Family Meal Fun

Assign roles in fun ways. Family meals can be a hectic time with many types of duties that have to be completed. One way of making meals a success is through assigning roles so each person makes a contribution to feeding the family. Roles can be shared. The beautifier, who is also responsible for the table setting and drinks, the cook, the vegetable chopper, the dish-washer, the dish-dryer, the table clearer/cleaner are all roles family members can assign and share. Not only does this help lessen the work done by the chef but it also teaches children valuable life skills in the kitchen. Roles can alternate on different days or weeks. Roles can be determined at the Family Circle.

Include favorite foods. Allow children to play a part in meal selection on certain days, or have a certain day where a favorite food is served. A Chippewa foster grandmother I know always had pizza on Fridays. The foster children in her care called it Friday Pizza Night and always looked forward to it.

The art of cooking. Have family craft night with the crafts being the food. Easy ideas for this include pizza with faces, fruit kebabs, or cereal necklaces. This way cooking is more like a fun craft activity. Teenagers could prepare avocado sushi rolls that look like caterpillars or flowers, or make tea sandwiches in different shapes.

Storytelling Time with food. Parents can bring their presence to kids as they did in the last chapter with activities that can turn into Storytelling Time, in addition to sharing a meal. If a meal is going to be part of Storytelling Time, set up at a time separate from the parent having other activities. There also needs to be flexibility on the parent's part with letting it turn out however it turns out and focusing on the process with curiosity and attention.

Seasonal Meals. At different times of the year, or the start of a new season, take a walk through a local neighborhood and notice if you see any food growing. Go to a local farmer's market. Find out what's in season, what's local, what's made without pesticides. Don't forget to look into things Indigenous people of the area survived on like nuts, seeds, and roots.

Have children gather the food or even help grow it. Making apple pie or applesauce with the apples picked from an orchard can be a good introduction to teaching cooking and making it fun for the kids. Apples in September, pumpkin in November, berries and watermelon in the summer are some examples of foods that can be picked by children in different seasons. Connecting them to where their food comes from and how it is grown is part of mindful eating.

Incorporate Rituals. Start the meal with a family prayer, poem, song, or lighting a candle. Gratitude is a nice ritual for beginning the meal, with a prayer or saying thanks for the food in front of you.

When I was a child and I had a nightmare, my grandmother would take me into the kitchen, no matter the hour and make a bowl of warm rice with milk and sugar. I remember the terror of the dream. Once I dreamed a bear ate my mother in a trailer. He ate the entire vehicle. I woke up very distressed. My grandmother didn't ask what the dream was; she just sat me at the kitchen table and fed me. I clearly remember sitting at the table savoring each bite of the sweet, warm rice, and feeling better. Sharing food together is a natural and powerful way of bonding.

...

Congratulations, you have completed Stage 4 of the mindful family journey: Mindful Family Meals.

CHAPTER 6

FAMILY RHYTHM

Everything in the universe has a rhythm. Everything dances.

—Maya Angelou

I used to think the future would look like flying cars, but now my imagination sends me in the direction of machine parts taking over our bodies, not to keep us alive but to program our rhythms so we can be "Better, stronger, faster" like the slogan from *The Six Million Dollar Man* TV show I grew up with in the 1970s. My hero growing up was actually the Bionic Woman. I worshipped Jamie Sommers so much that I carved her initials on the underside of my family's kitchen table when I was eleven. She was independent, capable, and while she had machine parts, she didn't act like a machine. She was kind and took time for people. Her machine enhancements helped her to be who she was rather than shaped who she became.

The drive for innovation in modern society has led to a worship of machines so much so that we see our natural bodies and biological drives as an impediment. Sleeping and eating get in the way so we've made processed foods that are quick but get us sick. We take sleeping pills because our bodies can't generate the right amounts of melatonin. Movement is reserved for going to the gym but we have no time to fit it in. One merely needs to stop and observe an average American city block on a Monday morning to witness artificial rhythms at work. People driving to work in traffic, taking calls, eating, texting, even putting on makeup. It took a worldwide pandemic to change this rhythm, but what are we changing it to?

Modern society isn't designed to fit our biology, instead it's designed for what's been defined as progress. Yet, we are living, breathing human beings who are deeply impacted by the people and environments around us. At the beginning of the book we talked about the train of modern society barreling full steam ahead to a steep drop-off. Artificial society creates its own rhythm and we're programmed from infancy to fit into that rhythm, even though it's out of sync with our own organic biology and what we need to be happy and at ease as human beings. We all are affected. When we develop problems or issues with our bodies or our mental health, we're conveniently told the problem is us, but no one looks at the artificial container we've been placed in as causing the problem.

This month's mission is to break out of that container and manifest some of your own rhythm. There are three tasks for this month. They have to do with the rhythm of the day, specifically the beginning, middle, and end. Beginnings include the intention set for the day and morning greetings. Endings are about letting go with gratitude, the importance of sleep, and bedtime rituals. The middle of the day is about how we move through our day and experience the moments, slowing down to provide space for our natural kindness and compassion to arise.

This chapter is inspired by two songs. The first is a Cahuilla/ Serrano song about Dragonfly, which I learned from my Serrano elder Ernest Siva. It is a lullaby and speaks to the importance of having a good heart. According to Ernest Siva, if you sing it with a good heart and dragonflies are nearby, they will come to you. If your heart is unsteady, they will flee. This song is the master guide for the rhythm of the day. May your heart be in a good rhythm. You may like to take a moment and listen to this song on the Dorothy Ramon Learning Center Website: Sing with Ernest Siva.

The second song that inspires this chapter is the "59th Street Bridge Song (Feelin' Groovy)" by Simon and Garfunkel, with lyrics that lend themselves nicely to beginnings, middles, and endings. Take a moment and listen to the song, if you can!

Finding Your Rhythm in Three Parts: Beginnings, Endings, and Movement and Moments

TASK ONE
Beginnings

Intention of the Day

The lyrics Simon and Garfunkel sing relate to things going too fast and slowing down so you can experience more of the morning. This is reflective of the morning rhythm intention. Mornings are typically a time that everyone is together as a family. It is an opportunity to come together and feel connected to each other before moving out into the world or onto the screen.

Yet mornings are some of the busiest times for families. There is a rush to do. That's the time I forget everything I know and revert back to habitual stress responses, raising my voice at my children, not being present with them in order to get dressed, make breakfast, get lunches, get the animals fed, get work material, and get out the door on time ensuring no curling irons are left on and all the doors are locked. This is a perfect time to water seeds of blame about whose fault it is that we're going to be late.

No matter how many parenting skills I have been taught about how to handle these types of situations, I often revert to my habitual stress response. It's like a path through a forest that has been built over time. To walk a different way means going through bushes and digging into hard ground. It takes more intention and I'm not even sure I'm building the right path to get where I want to go. It's much easier to go down a well-worn path and, for the most part, it gets us out of the house and to school and work on time, or sort of on time.

If my goal was to send my family off into the day with increased stress hormones and feelings of disconnection, the path of rushing and forcing would be great. But, if I want to send them out in the world feeling loved, with caring hearts, I need to do something different. That's where remembering my North Star comes in. Before anything else, I have to set a Rhythm Intention for the day.

DAILY RHYTHM INTENTION SETTING

Spend one to five minutes in the morning before things get going and notice your breathing (even one breath in and out) and let a rhythm intention for the day naturally arise. If nothing does, here are a few you can use, or pull a line from your North Star.

"May I be peaceful and at ease."

"May I offer fun and happiness to others."

"May others feel my kindness and patience."

"May I be curious and in awe of the people around me."

"May I reflect the light in others so they can see it in themselves."

Mindful Morning Greeting

Routines can help set the rhythm for the family as well as simplify life down to the essentials. From the Cahuilla/ Serrano Dragonfly's Song we learn to stop and sing, "Ush Kana," to greet the Dragonfly and if our heart is in a good place, the dragonfly will come near. We can also apply this to our children. One important routine is the morning greeting. American Indian psychologist Dolores BigFoot first taught me the importance of the morning greeting. "Greet your children in the morning with their Indian name so they remember who they are."

When your children are near, stop and greet them with a sound they like to hear. Do you have a special name for your child? Greet them with this name or use their proper name.

MINDFUL MORNING GREETING
In the morning when you see each family member for the first time, stop what you are doing, notice one breath in your body as you breathe in, and notice the person in front of you as you breathe out.

Then greet that person with a smile.

We are not machines. My coffee maker isn't affected by the temperature or noise or people in the kitchen, but I am. Whatever energy you are feeling as you greet your child, they will also feel. Intentions and morning greetings begin a rhythm for the day. I get up early and work on activities that require a high level of concentration. My focus goes deep into the work I'm doing. It's hard for me to pull out of that focus and acknowledge anyone in front of me. When I am practicing stopping what I'm doing and giving my full attention to who is in front of me (Child as a Mindfulness Bell), I notice I feel happier.

There was a study done by Dr. Matthew Killingsworth at Harvard, in which he used an app and asked several thousand people at various points in the day what they were doing—if their mind was in what they were doing, and how happy they were. He found that regardless of what people were doing, if their mind was in what they were doing, they rated themselves as happier. Dividing my attention between writing and greeting leaves me feeling unsatisfied. Stopping and focusing on greeting my family member takes intention for me but results in a better feeling within myself and for my family.

TASK TWO

Endings

Now we will turn to winding down rhythms, setting the tone for ending our day.

Sleep

Sleep is an area where we can get out of rhythm with our bodies' needs. Eighty percent of adults believe you cannot get enough sleep and be successful at your job (survey referenced in *The Promise of Sleep* by William Dement) yet sleep is critical to vitality in life, physical health, and daily rhythm.

Getting enough sleep at night is associated with mortality levels, according to the American Cancer Society. A Finnish study showed a link between good sleep and good health. Poor sleepers aged thirty-six to fifty were six-and-a-half times more likely to have health problems, and female sleepers were three and half times more likely to have health problems. Sleep problems among children and adolescents are associated with more behavioral problems, more learning problems, mood and emotion problems, and obesity (Montgomery-Downs et al. 2014). A study funded by the Centers for Disease Control in 2014 found that teens who don't get enough sleep learn less, have more auto accidents, are more likely to use drugs, and are at increased risk for developing sleep disorders (Wahlstrom).

Circadian rhythms are natural internal patterns of sleepiness and alertness that are governed by our biological clock and they are influenced by light and dark. Photoreceptors in the retina sense light and dark, and this aligns with our circadian rhythms telling us to be awake in the morning and go to sleep at night. Even small electronic devices emit light, so something like texting can lead to sleep rhythm disruptions. Interestingly, for teens the circadian rhythm dips between 3:00 and 5:00 a.m. and 2:00 and 5:00 p.m. With sleep deprivation, the dips can last to until ten in the morning. Teens actually get more energy later at night, making early bedtime difficult. It's not going to bed early that's vital for teens; it's staying in bed later, and to make matters worse, at puberty levels of the sleep-inducing hormone melatonin drop even lower.

We have different sleep patterns at different ages, yet society operates in a way that teenagers have to follow adults' sleeping patterns. Teens have their own biological rhythm. Ten hours a night is ideal for both teens and children according to the National Sleep Foundation. With the amount of electronics in today's world, school start times, and homework demands, it's no wonder that our youth are sleep deprived.

Bedtime Rituals

Having consistent bedtime rituals supports healthy sleep patterns.

Bedtime Ritual #1: Gratitude Practice. Ease into the night with a gratitude practice.

NIGHTLY BEDTIME GRATITUDE PRACTICE

Spend one to five minutes at bedtime and notice your breathing.
Let one to three gratitudes for the day naturally arise.
These can be things like . . .
"I'm grateful for my arms (or my ears, eyes, or liver)."
"I'm grateful I noticed the sunrise (or sunset or a flower) today."
"I'm grateful for my family."
"I'm grateful for my life."

Bedtime Ritual #2: Lullaby. Another bedtime ritual is a lullaby. Lullabies are something we sing to infants but stop as our children get older. Research shows that folk lullabies from the child's culture sung by family members help to regulate the nervous system of premature infants. I suspect they can help adults also.

LULLABY PRACTICE

Choose a lullaby type song and sing it before bedtime. This can be done with family members or alone.

Focus on the words of the song.

Focus on the vibration of the singing as you feel it in your body.

Start at a regular rhythm and slow down the singing as you focus on the feeling of the vibration in your body.

Bedtime Ritual #3: Mindfulness Practice. Counting breaths is another good practice to steady the mind so the body can ease into sleep.

COUNTING BREATHS FOR SLEEP

Lie down in a comfortable position and notice where your body makes contact with the bed. Notice the sensations in your body, the mood tone present, the quality of your thoughts in terms of racing, foggy, calm. Don't try to change anything, just notice.

Then, bring your attention to the quality of your breath. Is it rapid, slow, deep, shallow? Just notice it.

Follow your breath in and as you breathe out, count one. Then continue on in the same way, counting up to ten.

If you get distracted, notice where your mind has gone off to. Label it. Then kindly bring your attention back to your breath and start over again from one.

If you get to ten, go back to one.

Bedtime Ritual #4: Set aside worries. If you are having trouble letting go of worries before bed, you could use pebbles and a basket. Each pebble you choose represents a worry that you place in the basket so you no longer need to hold it. The time for solving any problem is when you are well rested and in a good rhythm, not before bedtime. If you really need to hold onto the worries, rather than pebbles, you can write them down and place them in the basket, knowing they will be there for you when you are ready to pick them back up. This practice can actually give a new perspective or solution to the problem in the morning.

Develop a relaxing bedtime ritual that supports your natural sleep rhythm. Start with one thing each week and build from there. Do this for your children and notice the impact.

TASK THREE
Movement and Moments

Slowness Practices

In the Simon and Garfunkel song there is another lyric about watching the flowers growing. We don't want to miss the moments of our lives. If we move too fast, there is a lot we miss and we are less kind. There was a study done at Stanford University in which students were randomly assigned to two groups. Both groups were told that they needed to get across campus to give a talk on the Good Samaritan. One group was told they were late and needed to rush, the other group was told they had plenty of time to make it. The researchers planted a person who was hunched over, needing help. Only 10 percent of the group in the hurried condition stopped to help. Of the group taking their time, 63 percent were more likely to offer assistance. Studies have shown that compassion increases our sense of well-being and it is good for other people. That is why we need to slow down. We will practice taking a Self-Compassion Pause and Mindful Walking to Slowness.

Self-Compassion

Dr. Kristin Neff, an expert on self-compassion research, identifies three important elements for compassion: recognizing that suffering is present, wanting to do something about it, and understanding our common humanity. We all suffer at different times, we aren't alone in our suffering, and there are others that suffer as well.

SELF-COMPASSION PAUSE

Acknowledge you are suffering and offer yourself compassion, not because you deserve kindness but because you are suffering.

Identify in your body where you feel the suffering and imagine it as a small child or animal that is suffering. If you can't identify it in your body, just imagine a small child or animal.

If you can find the sensations in your body, hold that part of your body as you say the words.

Imagine holding that animal or child and offer kind words.

"I'm here for you."

"I care about your suffering."

"May you be free from your pain."

"I will not leave you."

Compassion is like applying healing medicine to a wound. Even if you can't fix the problem, just bearing witness to it is sometimes enough to relieve pain or give more space to the experience to get through the moment.

Mindful Walking to Slowness

Most of us walk in doing mode, with a goal in mind, to get somewhere, or to burn up calories. Mindful walking is about being, paying attention to the sensations of walking, walking without purpose, being curious about the experience of walking. It's a practice for life that relates to living not to get somewhere but to stop and experience this moment of your life as it is unfolding.

This month you will practice slowing down in walking. Your slow may be fast compared to my slow. Trust your body to find your own rhythm with this and walk with nowhere to go.

KICKING OFF THE COBBLESTONES: WALKING TO SLOWNESS
Begin by standing tall like a mountain, spine straight, feet hip distance apart, shoulders back but relaxed.

Take a few breaths in this position, feeling your feet connect down to the earth.

Slowly shift your weight onto your right foot and notice how your body accommodates this position. Continue this process going to the left, then forward to the point where you can still stay balanced, and then back.

Start to walk. Pay attention to each step you take, the experience of your body weight shifting onto your right foot, to your left foot rising then moving forward and resting back down, while your weight shifts to your left foot, and your right foot raises.

Start with walking quickly then gradually slow down.

Find the rhythm that feels right for you to walk mindfully through life, noticing each moment.

Walk to Connect with the Earth's Natural Rhythm

Nature helps us awaken our instincts and can help us get in touch with natural rhythms. Do your mindful walk in nature. The journey to get more in sync with our own rhythms is tied with getting in sync with natural rhythms, in the earth, the days, and the seasons. As we get more in sync with our planet, we will get more in sync with ourselves and vice versa.

You can also try mindful walking barefoot. The electrical connectivity with the earth is grounding for humans. Research shows that walking barefoot has health benefits. It can change the electrical activity in the brain and moderate heart rate variability. The *Journal of Alternative and Complementary Medicine* found that it increased the surface charge of red blood cells, decreasing clumping and blood viscosity. This plays a major part in heart disease. Another study in this same journal found that earthing, connecting the body with the earth during sleep, normalizes cortisol rhythm and improves sleep. Connecting to the earth normalizes our body's rhythms. The earth is our ally.

Move as a Family

Our artificial society is designed for us to sit in chairs, in car seats, at desks, and many of us spend our waking hours in these positions. Our bodies are not designed for us to spend long hours in these positions. I was at the Interpersonal Neurobiology Conference at UCLA with psychiatrist and author Dan Siegel where he encouraged people to stand for the conference because sitting is being labeled as the new smoking. It has negative health effects. According to Dr. James Levine at the Mayo Clinic, we increase our risk of death from any kind of disease by 50 percent from sitting too much. Sitting actually increases our risk of cardiovascular disease by 125 percent.

The Centers for Disease Control says that adults need two-and-a-half hours a week of moderate activity or seventy-five minutes a week of intense activity, with two days of muscle strengthening. Older adults need three hundred minutes a week, with muscle strengthening twice a week. Children, at a minimum, should get sixty minutes of physical activity a day. Yet, even though we know this, we don't build physical movement into our daily lives in a natural, joyful way!

Think about our children and teenagers, whose active bodies are telling them to move, and yet we stick them at desks for most of their day. My child's middle school has them write papers about sports for physical education, as opposed to moving for the three days a week they have class. Even if they are going to play a sport for the day such as volleyball or basketball, by the time they dress out and dress back, there is little time for an actual workout.

Obesity affects one in six children in the United States. One out of eleven people in the United States has diabetes, and diabetes rates related to weight are growing among youth. Exercise and increased activity level can bring these numbers down. Families exercising together can be a successful way of establishing healthy habits and building back the natural rhythm of movement into your life. This can include family walks, family dancing, or family games such as tag or sports.

Cultivate rhythm together through family dancing.

FAMILY DANCING

Self-Dancing: Start with finding your own movement through moving authentically in whatever way your body wants to move. Don't worry about what it looks like from the outside. Authentic movement is moving from the inside. You can do this with or without music. It's typically done with eyes closed and an inner focus, exploring spontaneous gestures, movements, and inner impulses in the present moment. Getting back in touch with natural movement is integral to restoring rhythm. Begin with five or ten minutes of tuning into the body and moving like it wants. Don't worry about doing it right, just notice. Connect with your impulses, your senses, feel your instincts.

Partner Dancing: You can work with your children on this through mirroring games. Have them do a movement dance that you follow as if you were a mirror image of them. Reverse and have them follow you. If it is difficult to follow, slow the movement down.

Family Dancing: Try this with the whole family as a scarf dance. Everyone gets into a circle. One person holds a scarf and leads the dance for as long as they wish. Everyone else follows his or her movement dance. When they are finished, they pass the scarf to the person on their left, who then becomes the leader. The dance continues all the way around the circle and can continue going for however much time you allow. Let this unfold and have fun.

Moving in and out of rhythm with each other as a family involves both supporting each person's unique rhythm and working to blend those rhythms together in healthy ways. Write a vow for your intention to be present in the moments of your life. It could be in the form of a song, *Slow down I move to fast, I've got to make the moments last . . .*

. . .

**Congratulations, you have completed Stage 5 of
the mindful family journey: Family Rhythm.**

CHAPTER 7

FAMILY PEACEMAKING

*The planet does not need more successful people. The
planet desperately needs more peacemakers, healers,
restorers, storytellers, and lovers of all kinds.*

—His Holiness the Dalai Lama

In a long ago time, a great peacemaker emerged within the Iroquois
Nation. He built a white canoe made of stone that could float on the
water so the people would know that he had Orenda, which is power.
He visited many people on his journey, including great tribal leaders
like evil Thadedeo and grieving Hiawatha. Hiawatha's daughter was
killed by Thadedeo. The Great Peacemaker established teachings of
peaceful relations and deep forgiveness. His teachings were so great
that, in the end, Hiawatha forgave Thadedeo, who then became a
new man. So important were these teachings that the people of the
Iroquois Nation buried their weapons under the Tree of Peace so
their grandchildren in the future would never know violence and
they invited all people to join them in the way of peace. This offering
extends to this day to all of us.

We will focus on family peacemaking using elements of the
Peacemaker story as a guide. Peacemaking takes time. It is recommended you complete this month's mission over two months. There
are seven tasks you must complete: clear seeing, calming, mindful
speaking, mindful listening, discernment, honoring, and forgiveness.

We will start at the beginning of the Peacemaker's story and the task of clear seeing.

Clear Seeing

One of the first places the Peacemaker visited on his journey was the home of a powerful, cruel tribal leader named Thadedeo who was known to eat his enemies. He was so evil that instead of hair, snakes grew out of his head. Rather than come to Thadedeo's door, the Great Peacemaker climbed to the top of his home and looked down the smoke hole. He saw a pot of water boiling over a fire. When the fire burned down, the water cooled and was still, so still that it showed the Peacemaker's reflection. When Thadedeo went to the pot and looked into it, he thought he was seeing his own reflection in the face of the Great Peacemaker. There were no snakes upon his head and his expression wasn't distorted, but one of great compassion.

"This is a great man," he said to himself. "Such a great man would not do the things I am doing." And with that Thadedeo gave up his cruel and brutal ways. You could say he was seeing clearly.

This was his intention, to see clearly, even if it would be awhile before that came to pass. We can also be like Thadedeo and have distorted vision. When we get angry, we do not see clearly. It is like looking into a boiling pot of water. Everything is bubbling and there is steam in our eyes. If we can stop and still the storm inside, all the bubbles eventually settle, the water becomes still and cool, like the water in Thadedeo's pot and we are able to see clearly once again.

When we can see clearly, we remember our direction—our North Star—and we are able to inform our actions by that great vision. The trick when we are angry is becoming still and waiting for the pot to stop boiling and the water to cool. If we learn to do this, we cause less harm for the people we are most connected to, including ourselves.

Because this is such an important principle (calming the boiling pot) you will be given four ways of practice, starting with Boiling Pot Practice and Mindful Flower Walking. These practices should be done regularly so there isn't a boiling pot of water to cool in the first place.

BOILING POT PRACTICE

Imagine a boiling pot of water, bubbling and steamy. It's hard to see anything.

Now, imagine slowly turning down the fire. The heat slowly begins to dispel.

Imagine breathing in cool air and with each breath you breathe out, you blow into the heat, so that every time you breathe out the water becomes cooler.

Breathing in through your nose, let the air enter your lungs naturally and then blow the out-breath through your mouth into the pot slowly as if you were cooling the water. See if you can breathe out slower than you breathe in. This cools the nervous system and helps still the boiling pot.

As best as you can, see if you notice the boiling water going from bubbling to simmering to stopping. When the bubbles stop and the water cools, then the water becomes clear. Stay with this practice until you feel cooler and still inside and then let your breath return to normal.

When we are angry or experiencing difficult emotions, our minds are like a pot of steamy, boiling water and it's hard to see through the steam. We can practice focusing on breathing in through our nose and breathing out through our mouth—blowing cool air into the pot until the water becomes still and we can see clearly again.

Gaze inside the pot of still water. Remember your North Star Intention. Let it guide you in your next decision to act.

The Boiling Pot practice is a great way to teach family members about dealing with strong emotions. It involves a commitment to not fuel the seeds of anger or push them down, but instead to acknowledge them and wait until the emotion has stilled and cooled to act. The ultimate goal is to be able to see as the Great Peacemaker sees, from a point of compassion.

Thadedeo did not change overnight, even though he wanted to. Endurance has to be built to still the boiling pot. When angry, most people feel they are calm after about ten minutes of stepping away from the situation, but it actually takes the body at least twenty minutes physiologically to calm down, and that's with not thinking about the problem.

A second practice that can help with calming big emotions is Mindful Flower Walking. Think of a tree in a storm. The branches on top look like they are breaking apart, and sometimes they do. This causes destruction. But if you look at the base of the trunk, or down even deeper to the roots, you will see there is hardly any movement. The trunk is grounded in the earth and holding strong. We need to ground ourselves when we are angry. That is why Mindful Flower Walking can be helpful.

MINDFUL FLOWER WALKING

Bring your intention to your feet, feel the ground underneath you. Notice the sensations of your feet making contact with the ground.

Now slowly begin to walk, noticing the sensations of walking. You lift your foot, you move forward, you place it on the ground, you shift your weight and then repeat this on the other side. Stay focused on your feet making contact with the ground. If the mind wanders, especially with thoughts, notice this and bring the attention back to the feet.

Every time an angry thought comes up, notice it and say,

"Hello angry thought," and then focus back on your breath and your walking.

After focusing intently for a few minutes on your inner experience and thoughts, allow your attention to broaden to notice the environment and what is around you. Do you see anything on your walk that gives you a feeling of freshness? If you do, stop and use Thich Nhat Hanh's words, "Breathing in, I am a flower; breathing out, I am fresh." You can use other words if they work better for you. If you don't see anything, imagine something beautiful and repeat the phrases. "Breathing in, I am a flower; breathing out, I am fresh." After twenty minutes of mindful walking and breathing in flowerlike freshness, notice how you feel.

Technically speaking, calming is difficult because of how our brain works. When we feel threatened, our fight-or-flight mechanism takes over, and our vision is narrowed. It doesn't matter if the attacker is a saber tooth tiger or mean words our child just said to us, our nervous system takes it all the same way, as a threat on our life. When our fight-or-flight system becomes engaged, the part of our brain (prefrontal cortex) that helps us evaluate situations with long-term vision, planning, and making decisions literally goes off-line. This is the part of our brain that helps us to see clearly and remember our North Star. That's why it can cause us more problems in the long run if we act before we calm. The Clear Seeing and Calming practices help bring our prefrontal cortex back online.

There are two more calming skills to learn. One is a practice for dealing with difficult emotions called RAIN from Michele McDonald combined with a practice called Removing the Object by Thich Nhat Hanh, and the other is a Compassion Practice. The compassion practice can be used when you touch the hurt that often underlies anger. The practice below describes the technical rationale for why these things are important.

CALMING WITH RAIN PRACTICE

R—recognize that there is suffering, and then name the emotion. Naming is a powerful practice.

Our amygdala, an emotion center in our brain, actually relaxes when the emotion is named. Neuroimaging research reveals that the right ventrolateral prefrontal cortex is activated in naming emotions and that may be the process that dampens the emotional response of the amygdala. Putting feelings into words alleviates emotional distress.

A—accept what I am feeling.

If we resist or tighten against the feelings, we often make things worse. It is like getting a shot. If we tense our muscles, the pain increases when the needle goes in. It's not that there isn't any pain with a shot, but the pain is worse with muscle tightening. If it's impossible in the moment to accept what you're feeling, you can focus on the resistance to acceptance as the feeling of focus.

I—investigate the feeling in the body. Notice the emotion at the level of sensation.

Emotions are made up of energy and they result in sensation in the body, such as stabbing, tightening, tingling. Identify the sensation in the body and focus on the sensation, noticing the space it takes up in the body, if it moves, changes shape, gets more intense or less intense. Keep your focus on the sensation in the body as best as you can, without trying to change the sensations or getting caught in a story about what the sensation means.

I used to feel extremely uncomfortable if I ate spicy food and my mouth would burn to the extent that I couldn't make it stop. Drinking water only made it worse. And then I allowed myself to actually feel the sensations of the burning chili pepper without the story of not being able to handle it. The burning sensation actually softened in my mouth as I brought my attention, and I noticed rather than a constant wall of pain, it ebbed and flowed until it subsided, and I learned I could sit with it, without doing anything other than giving it my awareness. This was a much better experience than identifying with the story of not being able to handle it and frantically looking for a cure to stop it.

N—non-identification of the emotion.

Realize that, while you are experiencing a strong emotion, you are not the emotion. You are so much more. It is as if you are a wave riding up on the ocean, thinking that's all you are, and not realizing your greater spaciousness. That you are really the whole ocean. If we drop red paint in a cup of water, the water becomes red and that's all we see. But if we drop that same red paint in the ocean, it's barely noticeable, because the ocean is so much bigger; that's like us. If we can touch our oceanness, we can find greater freedom.

REMOVING THE OBJECT
To remove the object, we notice it is there at the level of sensation, again not the story about it, and after a few seconds, we let it go. We can focus on a neutral or pleasant part of our body and the sensations that are there, like our wrist or our hand, or we can focus on the breath. We only hold the unpleasant event for five to twenty seconds. We can go back and forth in this manner: Touching the painful part, experiencing it, and then letting it go and shifting to a neutral or pleasant part of our body.

If the situation is still too overwhelming, you can open your eyes and orient to the external environment. To orient, you open your eyes and follow your instincts to what grabs your attention.

Notice the color, shapes, or textures of the object you are looking at. This calms your amygdala, and lets your lower brain know that you are not in immediate threat of dying from a saber tooth tiger.

We do these practices because peacemaking involves first bringing peace to ourselves. When the Great Peacemaker met Hiawatha, he saw the suffering in the great man's eyes. Hiawatha was a good man. In spite of his own tragedy with his daughter being killed, when he heard the peace teachings, he accepted them because he wanted the violence to end. He took the teachings to his leaders and from there took them out into other tribal communities. Hiawatha couldn't have brought the peace to others if he hadn't learned to find it within himself first. This compassion practice can help with touching peace even among our strongest difficulties.

COMPASSION PRACTICE
Sit comfortably and follow a few natural breaths in and out. Once you have tapped into your natural rhythm, bring to mind someone you know who is suffering and to whom you want to bring some ease. Offer the phrases,

> *"I see that you are suffering.*
> *I care about your suffering.*
> *I wish you to be free from pain and suffering.*
> *I wish for you to be at peace."*

Now call to mind a difficult situation you are dealing with (it could be, my child just yelled at me). Once you have this scenario in mind, feel it in your body. Where does it reside? You can place your hand gently on this place if you wish and talk in a loving tone of voice as if it were your baby:

"Dear (your name),
I know that you are suffering. I care about your suffering. I am here for you. I am so sorry you have to experience this right now. I wish for you to be at peace."

Breathe into that part of your body, softening around the edges.

You can also call to mind other people who may suffer from the same situation you are in, understanding our common humanity and that you are not alone. And offer the phrases to them.

"I see that you are suffering. I care about your suffering. I wish you to be free from pain and suffering. I wish for you to be at peace."

You can then turn to the person that has caused you suffering, trying to see the situation from their perspective and offer the phrases,

"I see that you are suffering. I care about your suffering. I wish you to be free from pain and suffering. I wish for you to be at peace."

Let whatever feelings are present arise, pleasant or unpleasant, and notice them with curiosity. The intention and planting the seeds of compassion is what's important here.

We've learned stopping and noticing in previous months. When we stop and notice anger is present, it is time to do the calming. Learning peacemaking is a process, which takes practice and reminders. When the Great Peacemaker taught peace to Hiawatha, he used *wampum*, in the form of different colored shells, each representing a part of the teaching. The peace teachings in this chapter aren't the Peacemaker's teachings, but they are informed by elements of the story. You can make reminders for your family of the different skills needed for mindful family peacemaking in the form of a string of beads using the different colors in the diagram below.

Once you have calmed yourself and touched your own seeds of compassion, you can see clearly. Then you are ready to enter into relationship using mindful listening.

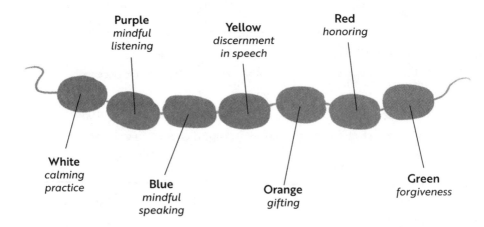

Mindful Listening

To truly listen takes practice. We first practiced this while building a mindful family ensemble. Here is another mindful listening practice. To begin with, pick a theme to practice with like things that bring me joy or a story of the day.

MINDFUL LISTENING PRACTICE

Start by noticing your breath for a few cycles. Imagine breathing in peace and breathing out all the negativity. Focus on the other person in front of you. It can even help to tune into their breathing.

See the person here and say to yourself, "I am here. You are here."

Take turns, with each person having five minutes while the other person talks on the theme, merely saying thank you when there is a pause, not offering your own ideas. When the five minutes is up, switch places.

Staying connected to the breath, focus on what the person is saying, without judging or fixing, just hearing.

After they finish speaking you can pause and digest what you just heard. You can also reflect back what they have said and ask if you understood correctly (i.e., "What I hear you saying is . . . is that right?"). This shows them that you were really listening and that you value them enough to give them your full attention.

After they finish, instead of rushing in with your story or a solution, take a few breaths, and give some space before speaking.

Mindful Speaking

Remember with Mindful Speaking there is no need to preplan what you are going to say. Connect with your breath and speak from your heart. We will go back to the talking circle for this practice. You can set a theme or each member can say whatever they feel needs to be said for their time.

MINDFUL SPEAKING PRACTICE

Form a mindful circle and pass a talking stick around from person to person. Each person speaks from the heart, letting needed words arise. It can be hard to trust the words will be there when it is your turn. When the stick comes to you, take a few breaths and let the words come from your heart. You will be surprised sometimes at the things you hear yourself saying, and the things you learn about yourself with this practice.

Speaking with Discernment

We don't want our speech to harm others. It is important to learn to speak with discernment, even in conflict situations. Before speaking sit in an upright position and take a few breaths. Connect with your heart before you say anything. When speaking, there are three helpful questions that Susan Kaiser Greenland uses in her program *Inner Kids*. These questions are: Is it kind? Is it true? Is it necessary? THese questions can be especially important to teach siblings.

WORKING WITH CONFLICT

In these situations, it is important that family members have engaged in some kind of centering practice first and that they slow down and use a more scripted form of communication. "I" messages keep the communication clear and truthful and are frequently discussed for these types of formats. The I message script is as follows:

"I feel [emotion] when you [give the behavioral situation]." It can be helpful to state whenever this happened and avoid bringing up multiple events. Just solve one problem at a time.

"I would like [list what you are wanting]."

The person listening reflects back what they heard and says, "Is that right?"

Then the other person can have a turn to speak using the same format.

Discernment in speaking is important. Only saying what's necessary and not giving too many words at a time that need to be reflected back is useful here.

For children, it is important to have an adult guide the process in the witness role. Ensure, first, that the children are calm enough to engage in the process. Remember calming can take twenty minutes to twenty-four hours.

There were times when Hiawatha brought in the peace teachings and he was ignored or met with hostility, some even made fun of him. This upset Hiawatha, but the Great Peacemaker told him that those people were not yet ready to hear the message. Rather than fight their resistance, he instructed Hiawatha to move on to others who were more receptive and come back to these people later. This is an important thing to think about when engaging in peacemaking, building the peace in little steps before moving to more difficult obstacles. When first teaching family peacemaking, it is recommended to practice with minor irritations or make-believe conflicts before working up to bigger problems. In families this can also include choosing the right moment to speak and making the ground fertile. For that, return to the practice of honoring.

Honoring

The Great Peacemaker first reflected the peace in himself. After that he went to others more receptive to the peace, such as Hiawatha. For Thadedeo to change it actually took many people changing around him before the manifestations of the peace finally took root and were evident in Thadedeo.

To create fertile ground for peace, show others your own generosity. Start with practicing kind acts in the form of gifting. Have each family member make a list of small things they enjoy receiving. The list can include small things you can do for yourself and small things others can do for you. With this list, you can make a gifting practice.

FRIENDSHIP AND PEACE GIVEAWAY PRACTICE

Start with the gifting list of twenty small activities for each family member.

Do an activity each day for a family member. Be sure to

alternate among all family members, and include giving to yourself for one of the days. It is important to give as a gift rather than taking score of what you are receiving.

Do this for a week and talk about the experience. It may be something you want to incorporate into your family life, periodically brainstorming new, small things you like for self-care.

Keep a family Gifting Log somewhere you all can see and share the gifts you like to give and receive from each other. First, gather together and share which gifts you like to receive. Here's an example.

Family Member	Mom	Dad	Gabriella	Dakota
Monday	coffee			
Tuesday		foot rub		
Wednesday			reading	
Thursday				playtime
Friday				
Saturday				
Sunday				

Mom: Someone makes me coffee, or gives me a foot rub, a back rub, or 30 minutes to have a bath!

Dad: Back rub, foot rub, or time to read for 15 minutes without interruptions.

Gabriella: Reading time, someone does my nails or makes me my favorite dessert.

Dakota: 15 minutes of playtime, story time, my favorite smoothie.

Over the course of a few weeks, see how many gifts you can give each other!

GIFTING LOG

Name				
Monday				
Tuesday				
Wednesday				
Thursday				
Friday				
Saturday				
Sunday				
Monday				
Tuesday				
Wednesday				
Thursday				
Friday				
Saturday				
Sunday				
Monday				
Tuesday				
Wednesday				
Thursday				
Friday				
Saturday				
Sunday				
Monday				
Tuesday				
Wednesday				
Thursday				
Friday				
Saturday				
Sunday				

This gifting can also be brought to the family community in the form of a Family Honoring Ceremony. We started the Honoring Circle in chapter 3 as part of the Family Circle. This is another way to do the honoring.

FAMILY HONORING CEREMONY

Hand out slips of paper to everyone in the circle. Have each person write one thing they admire, a compliment, about each person in the circle.

Once this is complete, one person sits in the middle and the family forms a circle around them, each reading their honoring statement to the person.

At the end, the statements are given to the person.

Then, the next person takes their honor seat in the center. This process continues until everyone has had a chance to receive their compliments.

Children too young to write can participate by drawing a picture of their compliment.

Generosity is hard to give and receive when feelings have been hurt. There are many pieces of the Peacemaker story that are compelling to me; one of the most compelling parts is the way the Peacemaker brings the enemy into the circle. Even Thadedeo is included. This reflects the true meaning of "All My Relations" and relates to a final practice necessary for families to maintain the peace—forgiveness practice.

Forgiveness

Hiawatha loved his family and suffered a terrible tragedy at the hands of Thadedeo. To some this would inspire warring and seeking revenge. No one expects Hiawatha to forgive Thadedeo, but Hiawatha knows revenge won't bring his daughter back. He understands Thadedeo is a man who had done terrible things and who has terrible suffering within him. Hiawatha is committed to the larger peace and knows the message of the Great Peacemaker isn't to punish but to bring everyone into the circle.

That's what we want for our family members and for ourselves—to be forgiven and to be brought back into the circle. For those who are skeptical, remember that Western science can back up the Peacemaker's teachings with data. Forgiveness makes us happier, improves our health, sustains our relationships, and boosts kindness and connectedness. In a study in Rwanda, war refugees were put into one of two groups, a control and a forgiveness practice group. Those that applied forgiveness to their oppressors after warfare had less post-traumatic stress than the control group. Emotionally abused women often have post-traumatic stress and emotional problems after the relationship ends. In one study twenty women were assigned to either forgiveness training or an alternative training in anger validation, assertiveness, and interpersonal skill building. Women in the forgiveness group had significantly greater improvement in depression, anxiety, PTSD symptoms, self-esteem, forgiveness, and finding meaning in suffering.

Forgiveness doesn't mean staying in bad situations, nor does it mean tolerating disrespectful behavior. It's about letting go of wishes for vengeance and even wishing well for the offender or reconciling if that's possible—though it's not necessary.

None of this is easy. It took a long time for Thadedeo to transform, even after he set his intention. When the Great Peacemaker goes back to visit Thadedeo, they find him crying out, "Asokekne-eh, it is not yet happening." His words make the water in the lake rough and troubled. The Great Peacemaker and Hiawatha tell Thadedeo to look at the smoke of every village rising peacefully around him. Thadedeo is moved to tears in a complete acceptance of the Great Peace. His hair is combed and his body is smooth. He is finally at peace.

If we can see each other's common humanity, our hearts may open and we will see that the circle is stronger when everyone is taken care of. If our actions cause a shift in the negativity in others to a more positive focus through an act of compassion, then our family is happier, our lives are more peaceful. At the very least, we don't add more heat to the fire.

The following is a discernment practice for apologizing when we have acted unskillfully. Remember that we are the adult and the relationship with our child is the most important thing (North Star Vision).

APOLOGY PRACTICE

Begin by calming the water in your own pot. Start with self-compassion for yourself by using one of the calming practices.

Once you have given yourself nurturance, do some perspective taking. View the problem through the eyes of your child.

Then apologize to your child for the unskillful way you handled the situation, or if you handled it okay, state it is difficult to have conflict between the two of you and you want to make things better.

Invite your child to tell you what has happened and listen mindfully, staying connected with your breath. Let go of right and wrong for the moment.

Reflect back your child's experience of the situation: When I . . .you felt . . . Is that right?

Later, if needed, you can address your child's role in the conflict, but only when they are in a calm state and for the purpose of teaching.

It takes warrior strength to be a peacemaker. Strong patience is necessary—it isn't about stuffing anger down, it's about rocking a baby through a storm until the winds and the rains subside. It is about seeing clearly and speaking and acting from a place of your true values, from a place that honors your North Star. One thing the Peacemaker says is that guarding the peace requires warriors with skin seven hands thick. Give yourself time and compassion as you learn to guard the peace within your family.

...

Congratulations, you have completed Stage 6 of the mindful family journey: Family Peacemaking.

CHAPTER 8

FAMILY COMMUNITY BUILDING

Humankind has not woven the web of life. We are but one thread within it. Whatever we do to the web, we do to ourselves. All things are bound together. All things connect.

—Chief Seattle

I was working with a client on a collage. She selected an image of a community of people coming together to build a dwelling using sticks and twine. The image stuck with me even into the next week, which was strange because I don't naturally gravitate toward groups, but here it was—an image that felt like belonged in my future.

In the mindful family journey, we have worked toward strengthening ourselves and our families. We have learned that the whole is greater than the sum of the parts and the uniqueness of each individual is critical to this. We are fractals. The next natural step is connecting with community, whether that is extended family, neighbors, or like-minded people. In this chapter, we will focus on community building.

Community building is something that we can grow into as we step toward it. We don't have to have the full picture of what it will look like already figured out. In fact, we aren't creating something from scratch; it's already within us and has been for centuries.

Community building, starting with an individual unit, is ancestral and it also happens in the natural world.

Let's take a lesson from African grass. In Africa's Namib Desert, mysterious honeycomb grass rings called "fairy circles" are spread evenly across 1,100 miles. No one is certain how or why these circles appeared. One theory is that termites form these rings. Another theory is that these grass rings independently self-organized into a circular pattern to compete for scarce water sources, with each unstructured group transforming into an organized system without any central coordination. When individual plants do this, they cause other areas to dry up. Others believe the rings may be caused by both termites and the grasses changing the environment individually, and collectively. They all need the same thing, water.

What if we as humans organized around our need for each other? This month's task is community building in such a way that we self-organize around our need for connection—the respectful connection I spoke about in the beginning of the book, *nindinawemaaganidok*—a profound form of interconnectedness with ourselves, each other, and the larger world.

Today, we live in a disconnected world. Loneliness has become a worldwide epidemic in spite of machine-based connectivity through the World Wide Web. Social isolation can be as damaging to health as smoking fifteen cigarettes a day. In the United States, a recent survey by Cigna showed nearly half of Americans always or sometimes feel alone (46 percent) or left out (47 percent); and 54 percent said they always or sometimes feel that no one knows them well. This pattern of social isolation has been building in our world for decades (Demarinis 2020). We need to form a different pattern.

The train of modern society has been headed toward a cliff and to get off the train we have to be able to imagine something different. My younger daughter, Sophia, whose name means "wisdom," said to me when she was in fifth grade, "As humans we can create anything and *this* is what we did?"

Let me say that again, "We can create anything." And just because things are as they are doesn't mean they can't be different. I have heard, "It's too late. The train has left the station." It's never too late. If grass rings in Africa can organize and create patterns, why not us? And if not you, then who?

There is a program for Indigenous people in the United States called Native Nations. It was started at Harvard University. My brother-in-law of the Cahuilla tribe stated that rebuilding tribal community has to start with families and branches out from there—smaller units growing to impact bigger units. If we build a pattern of connection in our own family, that pattern can become a fractal of positive change that grows as a repeating pattern in extended families, moving to community families, then into larger society.

When we start out at this, we will likely be the anomaly. We are repeating patterns of our ancestors (fractals), which includes our Indigenous ancestors. How can we self-organize individually and then link together to form circles of care fractals that manifest as repeating patterns in the environment? We will start with a restorative practice then take our stopping, noticing, and caring skills into relational mindfulness.

Restorative Practice

This is big work, so let's start with an individual restorative practice. This practice is called Body Scan and rather than the focus being on your breath, it is on sensations in different parts of your body, constantly practicing engaging and then disengaging. Body scanning can be done with a brief scan for ten minutes or over a longer forty-five-minute period. I suggest starting with a fifteen-minute practice.

You can have someone read this to you, memorize it for yourself, or listen to the guided body scan practice on the website.

BODY SCAN

Begin this practice by lying down in a comfortable position on your back. Notice the natural flow of your breath as you breathe in and out. Take a few deep breaths and notice the impact on your body. Return to your natural breathing, following your in-breath and your out-breath for a few cycles.

Now feel your breath as it enters your nostrils or mouth, travels down through your lungs and into your abdomen, and continue sensing down your left leg, and into your left big toe.

Bring your attention to the sensations in your left big toe, like tingling, vibrating, numbness, heat, cold, tightness, looseness. If you can't feel anything, that's okay too. Just bring a curious attitude to what's available to you to notice in this moment.

Now turn your attention to your little toe on the left foot, noticing any sensations. And then notice all the toes in between, perhaps as individual toes or one big blob.

Turn your attention to the bottom of our foot. Breathe into the bottom of your foot. Turn your attention to the top of your foot and your ankle. See if you can sense into your ankle bone. Then let go and bring your attention to your calf and shin bone. Breathe into your lower leg.

If your attention wanders, notice where it goes and then non-judgmentally, kindly bring your attention back to the part of the body in focus. Continue in this way going to your left knee, then thigh, then groin area and hips.

Repeat the process on the right side, starting with the right big toe. Move to the lower back, then the abdomen and gut.

If other body sensations pull your focus away, you can breathe into them and notice them at the level of sensation, not story, and then when ready bring your attention back to the area of the body you are focusing on.

Next, place your awareness on your spine, upper back, and around to your chest. Then shoulders. From there go to the finger and thumb, palms and top of the hand, wrists, forearms, elbows, upper arms, back to shoulders. Turn to the neck, the jaw, lips, and tongue, all the parts of the face up to the top of the crown.

Once you have scanned each area, imagine releasing all the stress and things you don't need through the top of your head as you breathe out, and imagine breathing in peace and ease as you breathe in. Then, let go of a singular focus, feel your whole body breathing. Allow your mind to go wherever it wants.

Finish with a few deep breaths.

Relational Mindfulness

In the children's story *The Velveteen Rabbit*, the rabbit's biggest desire is to become a real rabbit. He actually gets what he wants but not from working in isolation. It isn't until he has been loved for a long time, so long that he is tattered and torn and his eye and most of his fur has fallen away, that he becomes real. He can only become real in relationship.

For community building, we will turn to a series of relational mindfulness practices. It is in relationship that we really become who we are meant to be. Infants need human connection or their brains don't develop well and they can die. We also die earlier if we aren't connected. We all need connection to become who we are meant to be—to become real.

Once again, we turn to something rooted deep inside ourselves, a wisdom that has sustained our ancestors, a strength that is also in our DNA. To listen to our instincts, we have to stop and notice, something we have been practicing all along.

You are a combination of your ancestors, your mother and your father, and out of that emerges your own life path. It is important to listen within to find your path in life. You can find this even if you know nothing about your parents or ancestors. It is from listening within and then answering that call to developing your talents and bringing those skills back as an offering to the community, that you become real. Each person has an important offering to the circle so your own self-development is crucial to the whole. Your life matters for your family. It matters for all of us. Each of us brings our own unique gifts and contributes for the health and wellness of all beings.

The skill of stopping, settling, and seeing is essential to finding your authentic path. Otherwise the chaos and story that modern society has written over you can get you lost. This month we will practice stopping and noticing together. Let's start with a stopping practice most of us are familiar with called Freeze Dance.

FREEZE DANCE
Put on some music and have everyone dance. When the music stops, everyone freezes and brings their attention to what they are noticing in the sensations in their body (where these sensations are most prominent). Then notice the freezing statues of the others around you. As you notice the people around you, stay connected to the sensations you are aware of in your body.

Now that we have practiced stopping together, let's take it outside with a relational nature connection game. This game was modified from a game called Eagle Eye that I played at a Mentoring Youth in Nature Training in the Santa Cruz Mountains. It is called Rabbit and Eagle: Still, Settle, and See.

RABBIT AND EAGLE: STILL, SETTLE, AND SEE
First practice being like a rabbit when it first steps onto an open

area. It stills its body, settles by breathing on purpose into the belly, and sees from a place of stillness (without moving the head). Practice being still like the rabbit and seeing without moving your head, using your peripheral vision.

Once you have this down, find an outside area with barriers to hide behind that can be seen from one spot.

Select one person to be the eagle; the rest will be the rabbits. The eagle closes their eyes and counts to twenty while the rabbits hide. From their hiding spots they have to be able to see the eagle. The trick is to see the eagle without being seen.

The rabbits must use breathing on purpose to still themselves like the rabbit. The eagle holds up numbers with their hand three different times to ensure players are watching them. The rabbits have to be able to tell how many fingers the eagle held up each time.

The eagle can't move from the spot they are in. When the eagle spots someone, they call out the location and the person returns to the eagle. After a specified amount of time, say ten minutes, the game is called and everyone returns and tells how many fingers the eagle held up. Then a new eagle is selected.

Relational Mindfulness and Generosity

When I was growing up, I had an Aunt Marion. She had the house everyone, adults and children alike, gravitated toward. She held parties and play events. Game night was a regular event at her house and after school you could find her in the front yard with some sort of game that all the school-aged children on the block would flock to. She was connected with the neighbors, and served as a hub for family support and community fun. When I fell out of the tree at eleven and broke my arm, she was the first person my grandmother called for help. She wrapped a magazine around my arm for support and stayed with my grandmother and me until I left for the emergency room. Aunt Marion always answered the call. She knew how to build community in a way that was family-focused and healthy, and enhanced her life as well as the lives of others.

Let's focus on two community-building traits Aunt Marion reflected: generosity and everyday thanksgiving. This month you are tasked with completing two relational mindfulness tasks: generosity in the form of a giveaway and everyday thanksgiving in the form of a gratitude practice.

Both of my daughters participated on a debate team in middle school. The coach asked me one day to help them work together. She explained that when they work separately, the judge is looking at them all and giving them individual scores based on each other's performance. If one person is worthy of an 80, the others receive 77 and 76. When they work to make each other look good, on the other hand, it raises all of their scores and suddenly they're all getting 80s. They win individually and as a team.

Generosity is better for our success than selfishness; this is backed up by science. University of Pennsylvania researchers found that being generous led to more success than being selfish in a game of strategy. In this game, as long as there were more than two players being cooperative, as opposed to dominating the other and causing them to receive a lower payoff, it benefitted everyone.

RELATIONAL MINDFULNESS PRACTICE: GENEROSITY CIRCLE

Sit in a circle with family members (at least two people).

Begin by closing your eyes or looking down and following your breath into your abdomen, steadying your attention on the in- and out-breaths.

Then call to mind a time you were generous. This can be a little or big act.

Open your eyes and tell the story of your generosity. Allow three minutes. If you end before the three minutes are up, your partner can ask questions about your generosity.

When the three minutes are up, the next person shares their story of generosity.

End with closing your eyes or looking down and following three breaths in and out.

Giveaway Ceremonies

For a sustainable model of community building we can look to the giveaway ceremonies of American Indian nations such as the Feed the People practice of the Cahuilla Indians of Southern California and the potlatch practice of the Indigenous people of the Pacific Northwest. We will use the giveaway model as a guiding force in self-organizing around community connection.

Giveaway ceremonies are powerful indigenous practices of giving. These practices were so powerful that they threatened Western assimilation efforts aimed at dismantling indigenous community connections to the point that they were outlawed. In 1922, Charles H. Burke, the Federal Indian Commissioner declared, "To All Indians, you should not do evil or foolish things or take so much time for these occasions. No good comes from your 'giveaway' custom at dances and it should be stopped."

I participated in an Alaskan potlatch held for a community celebration. Each person brought a special item and placed it on the table. When it was time, we each went to the table and took an item. I was gifted with homemade preserves. When I think of Alaska Natives, I feel warmth in my chest and I think of kindness.

When within a tribal community people were jealous and fighting one another, a Cahuilla elder told my husband that he needed to feed the people to address the hurting that was happening. The elder hosted an event where he got people together to provide food and invited the community to a meal. Feeding the People helped restore balance among the community and oriented people back to working together in relationship with themselves, each other, and the spiritual realm.

Giveaways in the form of Feed the People or potlatchs can also be held for important rites of passage, signs of support, and for funeral anniversaries. If people are feeling down, a potlatch can lift their spirits. If communities are troubled, a giveaway can offer healing. If communities are fighting, Feed the People can restore harmony and balance. Giveaways help build new relationships and sustain old ones.

In *Guests Never Leave Hungry*, the autobiography of James Sewid, a Kwakiutl Indian chief who was born in 1910 and lived in British Columbia, Sewid speaks of the difficulty of living in both the white and Indian worlds at a time when such sacred giving was forbidden by the authorities. One of the triumphs of his story is his success in bringing back the custom that had been "outlawed and lost." "Always Giving Away Wealth" is, in fact, the title of one of his book's chapters.

Studies reveal health benefits for older people who give. One hundred and twenty-eight older adults aged sixty-five to eighty-five were given forty dollars a week for three weeks. They were randomly assigned to either spend the money on themselves or on others. Then they had their blood pressure, which is predictive of important health outcomes, measured. The people who spent money on others had a significant decrease in blood pressure at a magnitude comparable to anti-hypertensive medication and exercise.

Inviting families over to share dinner can be an informal Feed the People event. My husband and I were recently invited to a Mexican American family's home It seemed a simple enough affair, but much care went into hosting us. We are vegan and they made us a vegan Mexican dinner for the event. We ate together and afterward adults and children played charades and a board game that went late in to the evening. It's a warm memory and provided conditions for healthy family interaction, generosity, and sharing.

PRACTICE GENEROSITY THROUGH A GIVEAWAY CEREMONY

Hold a Family Circle and brainstorm a giveaway celebration and gifts of no cost or low cost that you can make. This can also include gifts of time and service.

Choose a theme and audience for the giveaway. There are many themes that can be used for the giveaway: as everyday Thanksgiving, to honor seasonal foods, to acknowledge rites of passage, to honor intermarriage connections, etc.

To hold the giveaway ceremony, lay items out on a blanket or table. People come forward, take something they like and then step back. Food can be served or it can be part of another gathering, Family Circle, or celebration.

Participating in the giveaway honors both the giver and the receiver. The people receiving set the conditions for the giver to practice generosity. The person giving sets the conditions for the receiver to practice Thanksgiving.

Give with no expectation of receiving anything back.

You might wonder about giving and not receiving anything back. It is important to give with no expectation of receiving anything. If your giving is creating harm for yourself or others, you may have to make changes or give in ways that don't bring harm. This is different than giving to receive. When the Peacemaker instructed Hiawatha to offer peace to villages and they were non-receptive, the Peacemaker told Hiawatha to leave the village peacefully and go to other places to offer the peace and return later to see if the conditions were better.

We may not give to others in order to benefit ourselves, but this is often the result. In a study in the Journal of Biobehavioral Medicine that looked at fMRI scans, brain activation was associated with individual differences in giving support, but not receiving it. When performing a stressful mental math task, participants who reported giving the most support had reduced activation in brain areas related to stress responses. In contrast, receiving a lot of support was unrelated to activation in stress-related regions. Giving higher levels of support was also linked to increased activity in a brain area that functions as part of the reward system during an "affiliative" task, in which subjects looked at pictures of loved ones; and during a "prosocial" task, in which subjects had a chance to win money for someone in need.

Volunteering Is Also a Form of Giving

In a review of forty studies on the effect of volunteering on general health and happiness published in the *Journal BMC Public Health*, volunteering not only improved well-being and life satisfaction, it was also linked with decreased depression and a lower risk of dying early. Another study published in 2013 in the *American Journal of Public Health* found that giving time and assistance to others reduced the mortality risk tied to stress, a known risk factor for many chronic diseases (Jenkinson 2013, Rogers 2016).

VOLUNTEER PLANNING

Brainstorm ideas of how you could give as a family. Start with each member journaling about different causes they would like to support.

Choose three from the family's list of ideas and research more about them.

Over the next three months participate in a volunteering activity. You could try all three as a family. Ideas could be partnering with existing organizations or starting your own tradition (neighborhood pie-making giveaway).

Hold a talking circle on your experiences volunteering and how you want to proceed with giving in the future as a family.

This can help make the family ensemble stronger, with family members working together for a higher cause.

Relational Mindfulness: Everyday Thanksgiving

In the Iroquois American Indian Thanksgiving Address, every aspect of Creation is greeted and thanked on a daily basis. The real Thanksgiving is a daily practice. All the gifts we have been given are remembered and acknowledged. We remember our responsibility to our communities and to each other. We give thanks, acknowledge our gifts, and from that comes a natural instinct to give back. Being thankful actually boosts generosity. When we reflect on what we are grateful for, we tend to be more helpful. In one 2006 study, participants who were feeling grateful were more willing to help someone out by taking a boring survey, than participants who weren't feeling grateful. In another study, people who kept a gratitude journal offered more help and emotional support to others than people who wrote about hassles or neutral events.

Gratitude motivates us. Pioneering gratitude researcher Robert Emmons explains in his article "Pay It Forward" that "Gratitude serves as a key link between receiving and giving. It moves recipients to share and increase the very good they have received." This even works with teens. Research predicts that when teens focus on what they're grateful for, they're more likely to give to others. Let's practice Thanksgiving relationally with storytelling.

STORYTELLING: GRATITUDE CIRCLE

Beginning

Sit in a circle, light a candle in the middle, and make a dedication to your ancestors.

Dyads Relational Mindfulness Practice: Gratitude

Divide into pairs and select a speaker and a listener.

The listener asks, "What are you grateful for?"

The speaker answers.

When they are done, the listener says, "Thank you, what are you grateful for?" (The listener says nothing else.)

After three minutes, switch speaker and listener.

After another three minutes, share about your experience with each other.

Group Gratitude Stories

Using a talking circle format, take turns going around the circle having each person share a story about gratitude.

In sharing stories about family members, remember to practice the Spirit of Respect.

Endings

End the story time with each person saying one word that stands out for them from the stories they heard.

Finish storytelling with the North Star Breathing practice.

Blow out the candle.

...

Congratulations, you have completed Stage 7 of the mindful family journey: Family Community Building.

CHAPTER 9

FAMILY PROTECTION DURING THE TEEN YEARS

This movie is about one thing . . . monsters eating children.

—Stephen Spielberg on *Jurassic Park*

It is dark when I get to the car. No one looks up to acknowledge me. My husband sits in the driver's seat. My thirteen- and fourteen-year-old daughters stare at screens.

"Let's go," I say.

My husband starts the car. There is still no response from the back seat.

"Seat belts on?" I ask, thinking no one else has to ask teenagers this question. When there is no answer, I look back. Their arms automatically move to pull the seat belt strap across their chests. Their eyes don't leave the screens. I wonder how they hear me with the headphones corking their ears.

The car is eerily quiet, except for the music my husband has begun blaring.

I look in the overhead mirror to the back seat. One of my daughters looks up at me with glossy eyes. My smile is met with a slight twitch, no sign of emotion, except maybe irritation. Does my husband notice this? When I tell my daughter to put the device down, she ignores me. When I reach for her screen, she pulls it angrily closer to her body, making sure I can't see what's on the screen. The more I try to track her device the better she gets at hiding things.

"This is my lifeline," she tells me.

Here in the car something feels terribly wrong. It has for months. Everyone says this is normal. I tell them my children used to open the door and run to me as I approached the car. They still say it's normal. I tell them my children used to have enthusiasm and curiosity about the world. They say it's normal. I tell them sexualized, drug-glorifying images from Instagram are being imitated in online posts from twelve-year-olds and their brains are being altered. They don't say anything.

I wonder if they know about the Windigo, because I'm sure something is lurking in this car that's not normal. I'm supposed to get that a phone is like a lifeline to a teenage girl. But I know that's what it feels like when you're infected by the Windigo. You need something to numb yourself while your life is being taken and you're the last to notice, until it's too late.

The old people of this land say the Windigo is a disease strengthened a long time ago by the white man, a cannibalistic spirit driven by greed, excess, and selfish consumption. My daughter says I'm crazy, but I believe the Windigo has taken up residence in the internet and it's attacking children's brain stems.

Tristan Harris, Silicon Valley's closest thing to a consciousness, says we're in a race to the bottom of the brain stem to capture people's attention. He left Google and focuses his work on stopping human downgrading. Even though he doesn't know about the Windigo, he senses it.

Three decades ago I was in Alaska hearing Native peoples' stories about their fears for their children who were riding snowmobiles into the woods, drinking, passing out, and dying. The children didn't want to engage with their rural cultural community. No one mentioned the Windigo there either, but they knew the high-stimulation, fast-paced images being delivered to their youth through their television screens was linked to the problem.

My husband tells me that he heard on the radio that developers of social media technology don't let their kids have the devices. When I hear this, I want to take the phone and smash it into pieces so it can't harm my children. Then everyone would call me crazy.

No one talks about the monsters. If you go back far enough, we all used to be told stories of how to avoid them; now we're told they don't exist. Instead of cautioning our children about the Windigo, we are inviting him into their bedrooms, our dinner tables, our brains. Monsters are just superstition, yet there's one right here in my car.

When I think of children on screens, I think of spooky stories. The world at your fingertips includes soul suckers in dark places and possession. This is a story about the monsters we don't recognize.

Many of the tasks you have completed have already put protection in place for your family. For this chapter, I am going to focus on things outside the family, zeroing in on the preteen and teen years. This is a particularly risky age, when our children start to go out into the world with less external protection in place. We hope they take our values with them.

This is also an age where they are figuring out who they are and they may begin to challenge parental belief systems. They push against us as they did in the toddler years but now we have less control and the stakes are greater. This is the age when we are more likely to see the effects of the monsters.

As our children enter into the teen years, they go through massive natural changes in body and brain. Teen brain development actually takes place from age twelve to twenty-four. It is a time of novelty seeking, emotional intensity, social engagement, and creativity. Their journey through this developmental period sets the stage for the core character traits that will lead them into their adult lives. Their developmental task in this period is to differentiate in order to establish an authentic identity that will serve them for their reintegration back to family and community so they can make their own significant contributions.

This is a tricky time because while they are pulling away, they also have this great need for belonging. Their need for belonging is a driving force during this period, and the types of connections they make shape who they become.

Let's go back to the scary story. One of the reasons we don't recognize the monster is that we may also be under its influence. None of us are immune to the Windigo. That night in the car I wanted to smash the cell phone. I felt the Windigo's hunger calling me, my thinking clouded. Before we were even out of the parking lot, I pulled my phone from my purse and clicked the round button. But that night it was different. I paused, took a deep breath, and remembered. I put the phone back. At least for that moment, I would not feed the monster.

What did I remember? Parents are the number one protective factor for the children at this age and peers are the number one risk factor. I have to maintain a connection to my child, and if I can see the monster non-reactively, it lessens its power. Because this situation brings such heightened emotions, I needed an equanimity practice. Pausing was my first step in fighting the monster; equanimity practice was my second.

Equanimity is mental calmness, composure, even mindedness, especially in difficult situations. An equanimity approach to safety helps give a wide-angled lens through which we can then make decisions. Equanimity is the thing that helps settle the snow blizzard so we can see more clearly. We don't naturally have equanimity. Naturally we go into fight, flight, or freeze mode, which in modern society may make our situation worse, because we act before we can properly assess long range consequences or desired outcomes.

To respond in a different way, we have to build an equanimity muscle, which is counterintuitive to everything Western society has taught us about being in control of our destiny. In equanimity practice we start with accepting things as they are. It doesn't mean we won't work to change something, but we will do it by accepting and seeing the reality of what is first.

EQUANIMITY PRACTICE

Begin by sitting in a comfortable position, upright and comfortable. Feel your body against the floor or the chair. Notice the natural rhythm of your breath, yet do not try to change it; just have a curious attitude about what it is for you to breathe in this moment. Notice the emotional tone of your overall mood. Notice the quality of the thoughts you are having. Is your mind busy, calm, foggy? Just notice whatever it is. Notice any sounds inside or outside the room, focusing on the tone, pitch, and the stopping and starting quality of the sound rather than any story.

Now, bring your attention back to your breath, focus your spotlight of attention on your nostrils, chest, or abdomen. Wherever it's easiest for you to feel sensation like tingling, vibration, tightness, relaxation, pleasantness, or unpleasantness. Follow your breath all the way in and all the way out; notice the pause between the in-breath and the out-breath. When your mind is drawn away by other sensations, sounds, emotions, or thoughts, notice that and then gently, kindly bring your attention back to your breath.

Follow the breath for about fifteen minutes, or longer if you want to.

Now think of a time when you felt even-minded about something, a sense of equanimity. Call to mind a situation that is causing you some difficulty. Don't pick the worst or most challenging situation to start with, but something with a mild or a medium level of irritation or upset. Once you've got that situation in mind and the different sensations it brings up and emotional tone, offer the following phrases:

"This situation is as it is. May I accept this situation just as it is. I am as I am. May I accept myself just as I am. You are as you are. May I accept you just as you are."

Adjust the phrases to fit the situation and continue offering them, while staying connected to your body and allowing whatever is there to be there. If it becomes too difficult, you can let go of the situation and simply return to the breath.

The Iatrogenic Effect and the Spread of the Windigo

Equanimity practice gives us a better chance for clear seeing. Accepting things as they are is our starting point. Once we have a clear mind and sight we can watch out for false stories and see our way through the trouble, relying on our North Star vision. The false stories I'm talking about here lead to a false versus authentic identity.

There is a story that has developed in our culture that parents need to step back during the teen years and peers should be primary. In their book, *Hold On to Your Kids*, Drs. Neufeld and Maté directly challenge this idea—they argue the opposite, that parents need to step up, because peer culture in America isn't about individuality and independence, it's about conformity and fitting in.

When I was in ninth grade, I got a haircut that I loved. It was akin to a Jennifer Aniston haircut before its time, with curls turned slightly inward. It wasn't the popular big curls, Farrah Fawcett haircut of the day. In fact, no one had this haircut at my school. At the water fountain a boy made fun of my hair and later that week I got my hair cut into something I hated but was similar to other popular haircuts. My hair would never look like Farrah's, and it took me until well into my twenties to accept that. That decision to fit in decreased my belief in myself and my self-esteem and allowed self-doubt to spread to my body. It wasn't until I grew my hair out and let it be straight, which is what it does best, that I made peace with my hair and started my journey of self-acceptance.

One of the primary ways the Windigo spreads today is through conformity. Both peer culture and screens promote conformism over authenticity. The transmission of values has changed from being passed down ancestrally to being spread horizontally through peers and screens. Our current society is set up to give more weight to peers and screens and less to family and culture.

It's surprising to find out that the generation gap we take for granted is a relatively recent phenomenon. For most of civilization, the music we listened to was actually the music our grandparents passed down. British child psychiatrist Sir Michael Rutter and criminologist David Smith's study, which included scholars from sixteen countries, linked the escalation of antisocial behavior to the breakdown of the vertical transmission of mainstream culture. This shift comes with increased youth crime, violence, bullying, and delinquency.

When I was studying at the Oregon Social Learning Center, my supervisor, Dr. Jerry Patterson, a leader in the field of delinquent youth, met with me weekly to discuss the latest research. One day, he pulled out a piece of paper and drew a line going up from left to right. The more unsupervised time teens spend together the more trouble they get into.

His research was replicated and top researchers found that putting troubled teens together made symptoms worse rather than better. They called this the "iatrogenic effect." This research finding, which earned Tom Dishion a merit award, was counter to mainstream thinking so it failed to gain steam in a broader context. The implementation of these findings never made it into programs in any significant ways in mainstream society in spite of the fact that it remains some of the most conclusive research out there around risk and protective factors for teens.

Your Child's Peer Culture's Impact on Their Authentic Identity

Best-selling author Dr. Brené Brown defines conformity as assessing a situation and becoming who you need to be for acceptance. This is different from the need we all have to belong. We should never be required to change fundamentally who we are to belong. That's how we give away our power.

Dr. Gabor Maté points out that while youth may retaliate against the norms of their parents, they're anything but independent when they're following their peers. In fact, their unique independence is sacrificed in order to fit into peer culture and become who peers, who have no interest in their long-term well-being, expect them to be. In spite of the myth of American individualism, our kids are growing up in a culture that's very much about conformity, and we're calling it the need to gain independence from parents.

For our children to be "independent" they have to first develop who they are. This process happens in relationship, through belonging. Rather than more peer time, children need more family time. They need their family as a North Star point of orientation. Prioritize that six hours a week of magic.

How Conformity Works

Conformity is associated with the medial frontal cortex of our brains. The term *conformity* is often used to indicate an agreement to the majority position, brought by either a desire to fit in or be liked (normative), which mostly has to do with peer pressure, the desire to be correct (informational), the desire to conform to a social role (identification), or the desire to please authority (obedience). As human beings, we have an innate tendency to conform, telling ourselves a story that this is the right way. It is part of our interconnectedness, in a way, to go with the flow. If we are living in a culture that values interconnectedness, like in a healthy ensemble where everyone matters and is valued for who they are, then this works well. But if that's not the case, then this tendency to conform is unhealthy and dangerous.

I am going to lay out a foundation for establishing an authentic identity and protecting oneself against the kind of conformity that leads to a false self. Legend says if we fight the Windigo directly, we always lose. If we fight our teens, we lessen our connection and drive them further toward their peers and away from the Family North Star. Without our protection, they are even more likely to fall into negative peer values.

This is an age where we need to be mindful listeners, hearing our child's voice as it's developing, and reflecting it back to them. It's also a time when we need to help them develop their personal North Star, which can serve as a personal marker set within the context of the larger Family North Star. For this we'll start with going back to the Spirit of Respect, which is an antidote to the Windigo. The Spirit of Respect will serve as a guideline in how to adjust the ensemble to meet the developmental changes taking place during these teen years.

For this month's quest you are going to be given six tasks to complete with your teen to promote family belonging and help set them on the path to an authentic teen identity.

These Teen Protection Tasks include:

- Respect for self: values clarification
- Respect for the larger world: volunteering and nature
- Respect for others
- Vision quest
- Skill development
- Family teen guidelines.

Six Family Conversation Topics with Teens

Teen Protection 1 | Respect for Self

There are two studies I want to highlight that reflect this tendency to conform. The first is a study conducted by Solomon Asch. In the 1950s, Asch conducted a series of studies testing if individual opinions can be affected by group opinions. His experiment involved showing college students a collection of lines and having them determine which one was the longest. However, before conducting the group test, Asch planted three of his confederates to purposefully point to the wrong answer. A large majority of the college students chose the incorrect answer because other people were making that choice.

How do we stand up against our peers when we see something different than they do? It starts with trusting ourselves, and that trust emerges out of self-respect. For this we need to go back to the values we started with in chapter 1, when we started our family visioning.

- Go back to the value worksheet and have each family member rank the ten values that are most important to them.
- With these values in mind, have each member write what self-respect means to them.
- In a talking circle format, share each person's way of respecting themselves.
- Whenever you see your teen manifest one of their positive values, strengthen it through reflecting it back to them, saying "Thank you for being kind," or telling stories in front of them about when you saw them embodying that value.

Teen Protection 2 | Respect for the Larger World

The second conformity study I want to highlight is the Stanford Prison Experiment, conducted during the 1970s by Dr. Philip Zimbardo. In the Stanford Prison Experiment, college-age students were put into a prison environment. Zimbardo's study used random assignment so that half the participants were prison guards and the other half were prisoners in a setting made to physically resemble a prison. Zimbardo found that the guards in the study obeyed orders so willingly that their behavior turned aggressive and abusive toward the prisoners. Within hours of beginning the experiment, some guards began to harass prisoners, behaving in a brutal and sadistic manner. Other guards joined in and other prisoners were also tormented. Likewise, prisoners were hostile and resented their guards because of the psychological duress induced in the experiment. As the guards' contempt for them grew, the prisoners became more submissive, which, in turn, helped the guards become more aggressive and assertive. They demanded even greater obedience from the prisoners, who were dependent on the guards for everything so they tried to find ways to please the guards, such as telling on fellow prisoners.

The experiment had to be shut down after only six days because of the emotional and physical abuse the prisoners had to undergo. The "prison" environment was an important factor in creating the guards' brutal behavior (none of the participants who acted as guards showed sadistic tendencies before the study). The situations we are placed in shape how we act toward one another and the world around us. They shape the story we believe about who we are and who they are.

One of the things both prisoners and guards lost in the roles they were placed in is empathy. How do we maintain empathy and connection to the world when we live in environments that promote form over substance and competition over cooperation and kindness is seen as weakness? Two things in the research that have been identified as being protective for teens: volunteering and nature connections; they both promote empathy and kindness. Placing our children in environments and roles where their best characteristics can deepen and manifest offers a superpower for this age group.

- Have a brainstorming session around volunteer opportunities if you haven't already.
- With teens' top values in mind, help them research volunteer opportunities where they can manifest and grow these values. Existing organizations you are already connected with may have opportunities, such as church groups or scouting programs.
- List some outings alone or together where teens can connect with the natural world (the environment or animals). Environmental nature centers and natural animal habitats often have volunteer programs. If they don't have much of a connection to nature, start with a picnic or hike in your area. Help them find unique ways they connect with nature. Brainstorm ways you can make even small nature connections a regular part of your life.

Teen Protection 3 | Respect for Others

No matter what, we need to keep our hearts open, the same way that Shinoh did when his son Nagah became a star in the sky in the story of the North Star. Shinoh's love helped transform Nagah into the North Star. Our love has the power to transform. If you feel your heart starting to close, go back to the Loving Kindness practice. Our children need us to be the North Star to help them navigate this amazing time. What happens now will impact who they grow into as adults. Maintaining their sense of belonging to the family is home base—something you want to come back to over and over during this time.

- In a five-minute free write, have each member write what self-respect means to them.
- Write five ways family members could show you respect.
- Share the writings with family members in a talking circle format.

Teen Protection 4 | Vision Quest

After connecting how the Spirit of Respect is relevant for teens and setting this foundation, it's time for some teen visioning. A future vision can serve as a concrete personal North Star, helping the teen stay focused on where they are trying to get. Values are connected to this and will help guide the teen toward what is most authentic and away from things that don't represent who they are or that put their vision at risk.

A vision quest was a rite of initiation in indigenous cultures that highlighted a passage out of childhood and emergence into adulthood. It gave them a place within the community. It involved mentorship, guidance, and was tied to their unique journey in life. We have lost these meaning-making markers or milestones for teens. This isn't exactly a vision quest but it is a visioning and will be followed by providing some mentorship around this vision.

Teen Visioning. Complete the below visioning practice with your teen.

TEEN VISIONING

Find a comfortable place to sit where you will be undisturbed, preferably outside and on the ground. Begin by feeling the weight of your body against the ground, feeling the places your body makes contact with the earth. Look around and notice what you can see ahead of and around you. Close your eyes and open your ears to the sounds around you. Notice the smells. Notice how the wind or sun feels against your skin. From this place, you can remain sitting or lie down and take three breaths, following each breath all the way in and all the way out.

Imagine yourself five to seven years from now out of high school. See what images or ideas come up. Don't think too much about it, see what arises naturally. What do you see yourself doing? What kind of people are you with? If you had to describe three qualities about yourself at this time in your life, what would they be? Can you see even further ahead, five more years forward? What are you doing now? What kind of people are you with? What matters most to you?

After spending some time with your vision, however big or little it may have become, bring your attention back to three breaths, all the way in and all the way out. From there direct your attention to the sounds around you. When you are ready, gently open your eyes.

Creating the Image. Following the visioning practice, have your teen journal about what they want for their future. Have them refine this writing and then create an image, a drawing (symbolic or literal) of their experience.

Honoring the Vision. Once this vision is established, hold a family ritual honoring it. One thing about vision quests is that it's not all figured out after the vision. Instead, it gives them a sense of where they're going and what things they can start trying out, many times in the form of experience and skills building under adult mentorship.

Teen Protection 5 | Skill Development

Older civilizations, which were more connected with natural processes, had apprenticeship programs where youth learned from adults. These mentorships were often based on skills observed in youth or their vision. We've lost that in modern times and it's desperately needed. If there had been an adult mentor in my life, then the hair-cutting incident in ninth grade could have been a key moment where a mentor could have directed my focus to skill development based on authentic identity as opposed to the shape of my body in comparison to magazine covers. I would have suffered much less in high school if I'd had someone who could see manifestations of my strengths and guided that development.

Feeling a sense of efficacy (that what you do matters and you can improve) in school and extracurricular activities, whether it's studying leading to better grades, or practicing a skill like music or sports leading to better performance, is important in this time period, linking to the visioning and helping to develop authentic identity. Now the vision is rarely complete at this time; it's something most of us grow into, so trying different things out can be a natural part of the process.

Involvement in skill-building environments provides an opportunity for other healthy adults to promote the development of values and skills and connects the teen to a larger community where they can develop their voice and feel they matter.

- Identify skills teens want to develop in the form of hobbies. This could overlap with their volunteering but should involve developing a talent, connecting with positive adults, and having opportunities to feel a sense of efficacy.
- Identify what setting or organizations teens could connect with to begin to develop these skills.

DINNER TABLE COACHING: THREE STRENGTHS AND ONE OPPORTUNITY FOR GROWTH

In her classroom, Dr. Brené Brown has people practice sharing three strengths and one opportunity for growth, and that opportunity for growth needs to come from the student's strengths.

Have your teen present things, even school projects, and use this format. It will help with positive focus—noticing what teens are doing well and generating feedback that helps people grow rather than shut down. This supports you in understanding your teen's strengths and how they can be used for growth.

Teen Protection 6 | **Family Teen Guidelines**

Having an individual and family North Star in place is vital for teens. We also know teens' prefrontal cortex is in the process of being developed. Because it's not fully formed, teens can be impulsive, dangerous risk-takers, and value the present payoff over the long-term gain. It's not that they don't understand the long-term consequences of their behavior, they just don't care in the moment. For more on teen brain development, read Dan Siegel's book, *Brainstorm.*

Family guidelines around risky behavior help serve as an external prefrontal cortex so that those fibers have time to grow and fully connect.

We will start with screen time. We would never put our teen on a motorcycle on the freeway at age eleven and say, "They can learn about street safety on their own." The internet is no different.

My oldest daughter was in the first generation of iPhone kids. In fifth grade she started asking about having her own cell phone; by sixth grade she felt like an outcast if she didn't have a phone and the popular apps like Instagram and Snapchat, even though these apps are age-restricted to thirteen-year-olds. "Even the fourth graders had Instagram," she told me. In essence, if I didn't give her a phone, I was making her a social outcast.

Screen time starts as a babysitting device or as a result of peer pressure, but it quickly moves to alterations in brain chemistry and neural wiring. Let's take social media. With social media apps, other people see what you post, and if people like it, then your score of "likes" increases. Whenever you get a like, post, text, ding, dopamine—a feel-good hormone—gets released. This affects your brain in the same way a slot machine impacts a gambler, setting you up for addictive behavior in which you check your phone more and more to see if you have more likes, or posts, or texts, or dings.

With social media use, youth are getting worse as opposed to better at social skills. A study at UCLA looked at the effects of screen time on youth identification of emotions. The study compared sixth graders who went to a leadership camp where they had no screen time to sixth graders using screen time as usual. They tested them on emotion recognition tasks before and after the camp. They found that after six days of no screen time, the non-screen time group improved in emotion recognition tasks over the youth who had screen time as normal.

Two hours of screen time a day is the maximum amount recommended for all screen time, according to both the American Academy of Pediatrics and the National Heart, Lung and Blood Institute. Yet, a new study finds at least 70 percent of American twelve- to fifteen-year olds spend more time in front of a TV or computer.

Prior to my children's teen years, we weren't a family that wrote policies but with what I saw in the car the night I became aware of Windigo, I was willing to try anything.

Hold a series of family meetings and write policies on screen time and other key teen issues. In addition to screen time and social media, critical topics for this age are unsupervised peer time, substance use, and sexuality. Help your teens understand that the more they follow the guidelines, the more freedom they will get, and the less they follow the guidelines, the less freedom they will receive.

If they falter, remember that they are learning and testing the waters. Problem-solve with them. List what they need to do, why they have a hard time doing it, and how you can help them follow the guideline.

The Unprecedented Nature of This Technological Era

I started this chapter with a story about how the Windigo has taken up residence in the screen. I was at a writers' conference in Idyllwild, California. After I workshopped my essay about the Windigo, a man in his eighties who had been very good at catching poor word choices and grammar problems said, "I didn't focus on words or grammar in this piece, I was so taken with the topic that it had me wondering is this something different than previous generations have had to deal with?"

It's easy to dismiss the angst we feel as parents with our children's fixation on screen time as something all generations go through. This is also a feature of the Windigo: getting you to ignore your natural instincts. We were a family who wouldn't allow televisions into our bedrooms and then screens exploded and not only do our children have Netflix in their bedrooms, they have it all over the house. It's literally carried from room to room as they brush their teeth, change their clothes, get something out of the refrigerator. How were we not on top of this?

Let me give you one more piece of research to consider. Dr. Peter Kahn, psychologist at the University of Washington, states that the intrusion of technology over nature in our lives and our children's lives may be one of the central psychological problems of our times. For almost all of humanity's existence we have had deep nature connections, and learned from nature about how the world works and who we are. We are now learning from technology and machines and it is impacting our minds, bodies, and hearts.

When we consider the extent that asthma rates rise from bad air pollution, buildings we enter warn that they have cancer-causing materials, and we are facing a sixth extinction, and we simply think, *Oh that's the way it is,* if we think at all, we have gone too far. If a child grows up in a home with violence later marries an abusive spouse, the violence is normalized and they may not recognize such violence as bad. We are normalizing the destruction of our planet because we are used to it and we haven't developed deeper connections with the very earth that our survival depends upon. By following through with these six Teen Protection Tasks above, we give our children a strong measure of protection that will stand them in good stead.

Reintegration

The teenage years can be incredibly challenging for families. In many ways, teens shine the light on all of our flaws and reflect them back to us in their behavior. It's hard to keep your eyes open and stay calm.

Even though our tech-based media often divide us, when operated with wholesome intentions, our screens can also bring us together by cocreating and sharing new global stories. I'm going to end this chapter with a story from popular culture. In the Disney movie *Maleficent*, the reworking of the tale of the Sleeping Beauty, the evil queen curses the infant princess Aurora with a death-like sleep that will come into effect on her sixteenth birthday from the prick of a spinning wheel. But Maleficent comes to love the child. The twist comes when Maleficent reveals the curse can only be broken with true love's kiss, but that there is no such thing as true love, and the princess appears to be lost to an eternal sleep. It isn't until Maleficent, in her grief, kisses the young princess's forehead and Aurora wakes up that growth takes place. In this film, it is the strength of family love that brings the adolescent girl out of the death-like trance of the Windigo back into life, saving Aurora and freeing Maleficent. The love between parent and child is what saves them both.

Through childhood and the teenage years, may you and your family have many moments of experiencing the connection between ancestors, parents, and children as love. It is my sincere wish that we awaken to a way of living and taking care of the people we love that nourishes us deeply. As we as families become more mindful and caring of each other, our culture and society will also transform, perhaps slowly at first, but with increasing energy and confidence.

· · ·

Congratulations, you have completed Stage 8 of the mindful family journey: Family Protection for Teens.

CHAPTER 10

BUTTERFLY WINGS

There is nothing like a dream to create the future.

—Victor Hugo

We are approaching the end of our journey together, but endings always bring about new beginnings. You've planted many seeds over the course of the year in which you have been reading this book and following the practices in it. Now it's time to let those roots grow deep. It is now up to you to determine what you will water and cultivate on your family journey moving forward. It is time to let your dreams create your future.

Take a moment and go back to where you started this journey. Light your candle and read your intention for why you started this in the first place. Review your maps (Family Continuation and Transformations Map, Spirit of Respect Map, and Cultivating Joy Map) and your Family Values Legend. Review your North Star Vision. Is there anything you want to modify or expand on? Hold a Mindful Family Visioning Circle and review your Mindful Family Values.

In an old Billy Crystal movie called *City Slickers*, there was a mean old wrangler that went around saying the secret to life was one thing. If I had to pick one thing based on both science and ancient knowledge, I would say it is connection.

Native psychologist Art Martinez said in a talk at the National Indian Child Welfare Association years ago that when we heal ourselves, we heal the ancestors that came before us, and the children that follow in our footsteps. Cultivating All My Relations gives our children, grandchildren, and great-grandchildren a foundation upon which seeds of happiness can grow and flourish, and strong roots of stability to weather the challenges that will come in their lifetimes. An ancient worldview based on respect of life of all things can help inoculate us against the unhealthy influences of colonized society, working toward building a future that is sustainable for all things.

Mindful Families is about wild sustainability, which breaks free from creating artificial environments that can't sustain our songs, our rhythms, our bodies, or our hearts. When Greek civilization was created, the people broke from all things wild, labeled them as savage, and developed an artificial world that lost sight of "reality."

The great empire and its systems that created the container we live in won't be the same ones to solve the problems of increased depression, suicide, and planet destruction, not without turning us all into robots. The way they solve problems doesn't sustain humanity. No, the ones that will change things will be individuals within families who change their fractal pattern and pull community toward them. They will break from the story of colonized society, and remember who they are. They will start small and grow.

There will be Goliaths that try to put up obstacles and tear these fractals apart. But eventually, like the African fairy rings and David, they will sustain themselves, first in isolated corners, but eventually they will grow, because there is no other option. If they do not find sustainability, the planet will not survive. Human beings will no longer be able to clothe and feed and shelter themselves on the back of Turtle Island, our home here on Earth. Artificial society is looking to technology for the answers to these problems. That means more genetically modified food, more electronic devices that modify our brains and limit our attention spans, robots for potential marriage partners, and even another planet to live on.

Have you ever heard that the flutter of a butterfly's wing on one side of the planet can cause changes thousands of miles away? That's what we're talking about here. Butterfly wings, tiny changes that can make an impact. While you focus on yourself, your children, and your family, and maybe even your community, positive impacts are being made—even if it's just five minutes of sitting meditation a day. You are the butterfly wing influencing change in a direction that supports health for everyone, because we are all related at the deepest level.

Pretty heavy stuff. I bet when you picked up this book, you had heard about mindfulness and were looking for a way to apply it in your daily life with your children. It was really for them, and here I am talking about changing the world for all of us! You have the tools to go deep into the woods, the instinctual world, and return home. *Chi Miigwetch*! Thank you for being on this journey.

Follow your instincts.

MINDFUL FAMILY QUESTS

STAGE 1: FAMILY VISIONING

Daily Practice
- North Star Breathing, five minutes, alone or as a family (audio track).
- Child as a Mindfulness Bell practice, every time your child comes to you, stop what you are doing, feel your breath, and notice your child as if you were seeing them for the first time.
- Spirit of Respect, fifteen minutes, don't worry about what others are doing and just focus on what you are modeling.

Activities
- Complete the Family Vision North Star Intention Cairn, and keep this where you can see it. WARM UP (Family Values); MAPS (Family Tree, Family Origins, Ancestor Continuation Map, Spirit of Respect, Cultivating Joy); LEGEND (Family Values).

Journal
- Family Story that brings out one of your family values (joy, respect, ancestral strength) and share it with your family.
- Begin a Family Stories Book that will include maps, historical research, interviews, ancient stories, current stories.

Nightly Reflection
- Mindful Family Values Growing Log, think back on the day, review your family values and enter the values you planted or watered today, and write your intention for tomorrow.

Expanding the Learning

- *Look Deeply:* Share the Spirit of Respect with your family. Talk about what respect means to you as a family. Have each member give examples of ways of showing respect. Have each family member paint a symbol of respect on their own stone.
- *Nature Connection:* Try a fractal walk with your family and see how many examples you can find in your neighborhood of repeating patterns. Talk about repeating patterns in your family.
- *Community Connection:* Bring it to the extended family or larger community. Invite extended family or several families together to share their stories of ancestral family values.

STAGE 2: MINDFUL FAMILY CIRCLE

Daily Practice

- Mindfulness Sitting Practice or North Star Breathing, five minutes, alone or as a family.
- Child as a Mindfulness Bell Practice.
- Find the Treasure Game: Designate a certain time period each day to catch your family member doing something you appreciate. Erase all preconceived notions you have about them and notice all the things that you like about them or their behavior in this moment. Let them know the specific things you appreciate. If it's behavioral things, be sure to offer the compliment as soon as they do the behavior, so it really sticks.
- Loving Kindness Practice as part of your sitting practice.

  "May you be filled with loving kindness.

  May you be well.

  May you be peaceful and at ease.

  May you be safe and protected both inside and outside.

  May you be happy, truly happy.

  May you be free."

Activities
Mindful Family Circle: Share Family Stories (joy, ancestral strength, respect) in a Talking Circle format. Include improv games reflecting the group guidelines.

Expanding the Learning
- *Look Deeply:* Talk about what ensemble means to you as a family.
- *Nature Connection:* Try a walk with your family and see if there is anything from nature that you would like to add to your talking stick or have each family member make talking pieces with these items.
- *Community Connection:* Several families could come together to share larger family stories.

STAGE 3: FAMILY JOY

Daily Practice
- Mindfulness sitting practice, alone or as a family, increase to twelve minutes.
- Child as a Mindfulness Bell Practice.
- Find the Treasure Game.
- Appreciative Joy Practice, also direct this to yourself. *"May your peace and joy expand, forever and ever. I am happy for you."*

Activities
- Joyful Moments Practice, five to fifteen minutes a day with your child, one on one. Set the stage so few rules need to be imposed on the activity. If there are rules that need to be established, let the child know up front, but keep them to a minimum. Gather whatever materials are necessary and limit distractions. Once this is established, shine the spotlight of attention on your child with a curious, enthusiastic attitude. Narrate whatever the child is doing, following their lead. You may join the play if they want you to with a "yes-and" attitude or

a Mirroring practice. Always keep the spotlight on them and follow their lead. Be a good audience. If play becomes aggressive or beyond established boundaries, return the spotlight of attention to your own breathing. If the disruption continues, calmly end the time and resume on another day.

- Family Circle, to brainstorm family fun.
- Six Hours of Magic, of time spent with each child.

Six Hours of Magic

Presence Time	Morning	Afternoon	Evening	Plant, Water, and Manifest
Sunday				
Monday				
Tuesday				
Wednesday				
Thursday				
Friday				
Saturday				

Journal

· Family Story, about joy and bring it to the Family Circle.

Expanding the Learning

· *Look Deeply:* Talk about what joy means to you as a family.
· *Nature Connection:* Try going on a walk with your family and see if there is anything in the animal world that you see expressing joy. Draw that image as a reminder to manifest this.
· *Community Connection:* Several families could have a community circle planning something fun.

MINDFUL FAMILY CIRCLE: JOY PLANNING

I. Preparation

· Appreciative Joy Practice
· Setting the Space
· Screening Out Distractions

II. Circle

Opening Ritual

· Set an intention with candle lighting.
· State Spirit of Respect Ensemble Guidelines (Honoring gifts—participate and bring your positive presence; Noninterference: Rocking Practice is allowed if you feel wiggly; Sovereignty: Right to pass, Respect others' ideas, Respectful Speech (is it true, is it necessary, allow time for others); Mindful Listening (two ears, two eyes, one mouth); "Yes-And" Attitude; Make each other look good; and Confidentiality (no gossip).
· State Agenda: Planning Family Fun.

Joy Games

- Play Mirror Game
- Play Pass the Focus

Discussion and Activity

Brainstorming on Family Fun. Nothing is too crazy.

- Individual Brainstorming: Write down ideas.
- Idea Sharing: Talking Stick format.
- Group Brainstorming: Talking Stick and "Yes-And" attitude.
- Consensus building. Selection: Select the top two or three choices and write them down. Then winnow the choices down to one or a combination of them.
- Plan: Write the plan on paper, including who, what, when, where, and how.

   Example

   What: A family picnic

   Where: The beach

   When: Saturday, July 26

   Who: The family

   How: Mom prepares food, Dad prepares supplies, Sister and brother prepare fun activities
- Review how the plan went at the beginning of the next Family Circle.
- Decide on next family meeting and roles to assign—Food Preparer, Note Taker, Facilitator, Space Setter.

Closing Ritual

- Gifting Game, making each other look good.
- Blow out the candle.
- Have snacks or a meal. Everyone helps clean up.

STAGE 4: MINDFUL FAMILY MEALS

Daily Practice
- Mindfulness sitting practice alone or as a family, twelve minutes.
- Add Loving Kindness or Appreciative Joy Practice.
- Child as a Mindfulness Bell Practice.
- Find the Treasure Game.
- Joyful Moments Practice, five to fifteen minutes a day with your child.

Activities
- Mindful Eating, have the first bite of every meal be a mindful bite.
- Mindful Family Meal, build the mealtime environment and make it fun. Use some of the activities for engaging children, such as assigning roles, picking favorite foods, using seasonal foods, beautifying the area, or making food an art project.

Journal
- Write a favorite family recipe or food from your heritage with a story about the food to include in your Family Book.

Expanding the Learning
- *Look Deeply:* Research a traditional food from your family of origin and learn about its history. Compare its health properties then and now.
- *Nature Connection:* Try an outing to pick food that's in season or visit a farmers' market in your area.
- *Community Connection:* Several families could come together to share a family potluck with dishes from their cultural backgrounds or with local foods.

STAGE 5: FAMILY RHYTHM

Daily Practice
- Mindfulness sitting practice, alone or as a family, twenty minutes.
- Include a self-compassion practice.
- Child as a Mindfulness Bell Practice.
- Find the Treasure Game.
- Joyful Moments Practice, five to fifteen minutes a day with your child.
- Set a Morning Intention, follow a breath all the way in and then all the way out and see what intention naturally arises.
- Mindful Morning Greeting.

Activities
- Family Movement, try a walk after a meal, a nature hike, or a game of tag outside.
- Family Dancing, try a scarf dance in which one person is the leader and the other people follow their movements. When they are finished leading, they throw the scarf to the person on their left, who then becomes the leader. You can play a mix of people's favorite songs.
- Create a Bedtime Routine, establish a ritual for yourself and your children.

Journal
- Write a vow for your intentions to be present in the moments of your life.

Expanding the Learning
- *Look Deeply:* Develop a gratitude practice before bedtime.
- *Nature Connection:* Try a Mindful Walk in nature. If you are feeling adventurous, walk barefoot.

- *Community Connection:* Do an authentic dance night with family friends. Take turns choosing the song and share your favorite music with each other! Use music that reflects the cultural background of different members and have a joyful celebration!

STAGE 6: FAMILY PEACEMAKING

Daily Practices
- Mindfulness sitting practice, twenty minutes; this can include:
    - Boiling Pot Practice.
    - RAIN and Removing the Obstacle practices when you are experiencing difficult emotions.
    - Compassion Practice.
- Child as a Mindfulness Bell Practice.
- Mindful Morning Greeting.
- Find the Treasure Game.
- Joyful Moments Practice, five to fifteen minutes a day with your child.

Activities
- Mindful Flower Walking: Walk for at least twenty minutes when you are irritated to find the freshness in the beauty around you.
- Practice Mindful Speaking and Listening as a gift to family members with five-minute turns on pleasant or neutral topics. Use Discernment.
- Daily Tending through gifting using the Gifting Log.
- Hold a Family Circle and Introduce Peacemaking Skills with Beads.
- Conduct an Honor Ceremony. Have family members write a compliment about each family member. Form a circle around each person and read them the compliments. This could be done as part of the Family Circle this month.

Other Fun Activities
- *Look Deeply:* Practice Apology with a family member.
- *Nature Connection:* Go on a nature walk and gather nature items to make your Peacemaking strings. Paint and string your item colors to represent the family peacemaking teachings.
- *Community Connection:* Invite other families into your peacemaking process and conduct a community honoring ceremony.

STAGE 7: FAMILY COMMUNITY BUILDING

Daily Practice
- Mindfulness Body Scan Practice.
- Child as a Mindfulness Bell Practice.
- Find the Treasure Game.
- Joyful Moments Practice, five to fifteen minutes a day with your child.
- Set a Morning Intention and give a Mindful Morning Greeting.

Activities
- Mindful Flower Walking: if you are feeling irritated or stressed, walk outdoors for at least twenty minutes and find the freshness in the beauty around you.
- Gifting Practice.
- Conduct a Giveaway.
- Conduct a Storytelling Gratitude Circle (this could be part of the Giveaway Ceremony).

Expanding the Learning
- *Look Deeply:* Talk about what Thanksgiving means to you.
- *Nature Connection:* Play Rabbit and Eagle.
- *Community Connection:* Do an outing with the family to volunteer for something you care about.

STAGE 8: FAMILY PROTECTION FOR TEENS

Daily Practices
· Mindful sitting practice or body scan, alone or as a family. Twenty minutes. Include an equanimity practice.

"Things are as they are. Let me accept things just as they are.
I am as I am. Let me accept myself just as I am.
You are as you are. May I accept you just as you are."

· Find the Teen Treasure Game. Designate a certain time period each day to catch your teen expressing a quality you value. Erase all pre-conceived notions you have about them and notice what qualities are being expressed in their behavior and link this to a value. Let them know the specific values you see manifested. This will help grow their identity around this value.
· Log time spent with your teen and practice deep listening for who they are becoming and reflect back the positive seeds you hear (Six Hours of Magic).

Activities
· Six Tasks for Teens Worksheet (page 169).

Expanding the Learning
· *Look Deeply:* Talk about ancestors or even historical figures who exhibited similar skills or values that your teen is discovering within themselves.
· *Nature Connection:* Try different nature-based activities to explore what your teen feels connected to. This could include water, hikes, ropes courses, or animal-based adventures. Because this is an age of risk taking, you could even plan an activity in nature that involves some risk taking and channel it into a path of healthy ways to take risks.
· *Community Connection:* Host a craft fair. Several families could teach a craft and provide mentorship as a community for the youth.

MINDFUL PRACTICES FOR YOU AND YOUR FAMILY

MINDFUL FAMILY MAPS
AND ACTIVITY LOGS

REFERENCES

Bissell, Tom. 2011. *Extra Lives: Why Video Games Matter.* New York: Vintage Books.

Hutter, Michael. 2011. "Infinite Surprises: Value in the Creative Industries." In *The Worth of Goods: Valuation and Pricing in the Economy,* edited by Jens Beckert and Patrick Aspers, 201–20. New York: Oxford University Press.

Lampel, Joseph, Theresa Lant, and Jamal Shamsie. 2000. "Balancing Act: Learning from Organizing Practices in Cultural Industries." *Organization Science* 11 (3): 263–69.

The National Center on Addiction and Substance Use at Columbia University [CASA]. 2010. "The Importance of Family Dinners VI." Retrieved from http://www.casacolumbia.org/download.aspx?path=/UploadedFiles/1intfzad.pdf.

Demarinis, S. 2020. "Loneliness at Epidemic Levels in America." *Explore* (New York, N.Y.), 16(5), 278–279. https://doi.org/10.1016/j.explore.2020.06.008.

Dement, W. C., and Vaughan, C. 1999. *The Promise Of Sleep: A Pioneer in Sleep Medicine Explores the Vital Connection between Health, Happiness, and a Good Night's Sleep.* New York: Dell Publishing Co.

Dyer, W. *The Power of Intention: Learning to Co-Create Your World Your Way.* Hay House Inc. 2010.

Eisenberg M. E., Olson R. E., Neumark-Sztainer D., Story M., Bearinger L. H. 2004. "Correlations between Family Meals and Psychosocial Well-Being Among Adolescents. *Archives of Pediatric and Adolescent Medicine.* 2004 Aug;158 (8):792–6. doi: 10.1001/archpedi.158.8.792. PMID: 15289253.

Eisenberg M. E., Neumark-Sztainer D., Fulkerson J. A., Story M. "Family Meals and Substance Use: Is There a Long-Term Protective Association?" *Journal of Adolescent Health.* 2008; 43(2):151–6. Epub 2008 Apr 11.

Fulkerson J.A., Kubik M. Y., Story M., Lytle L., Arcan C. 2009. "Are There Nutritional and Other Benefits Associated with Family Meals among At-Risk Youth?" *Journal of Adolescent Health*. 2009; 45(4):389–95. Epub 2009 May 28.

Fulkerson J. A., Story M., Mellin A., Leffert N., Neumark-Sztainer D., French S. A. "Family Dinner Meal Frequency and Adolescent Development: Relationships with Developmental Assets and High-Risk Behaviors." *Journal of Adolescent Health*. 2006;39(3):337–45. Epub 2006 Jul 10.

Graham, E., and Crossan, C. 1996. "Too Much To Do, Too Little Time." *Wall Street Journal*, March 8, 1996, R1–R4.

Grant, A. 2014. *Give and Take. Why Helping Others Drives our Success*. New York: Penguin Books.

Gottman, J. *Why Marriages Succeed or Fail: And How You Can Make Yours Last*. New York: Simon & Schuster. 1994.

Hamilton, J. 2014. "Scientists Say Child's Play Helps Build a Better Brain." Morning Edition. August 6, 2014. https://www.npr.org/sections/ed/2014/08/06/336361277/scientists-say-childs-play-helps-build-a-better-brain

Hammons A. J., Fiese B. H. 2011. "Is Frequency of Shared Family Meals Related to the Nutritional Health of Children and Adolescents?" Pediatrics. 2011 Jun;127(6):e1565-74. doi: 10.1542/peds.2010–1440. Epub 2011 May 2. PMID: 21536618; PMCID: PMC3387875.

Higgs S., Jones A. "Prolonged Chewing at Lunch Decreases Later Snack Intake." *Appetite*. 2013 Mar; 62:91–5. doi: 10.1016/j.appet.2012.11.019. Epub 2012 Nov 30. Erratum in: Appetite. 2017 Sep 1;116:616. PMID: 23207188.

Houston-Price C., Butler L., Shiba P. 2009. "Visual Exposure Impacts on Toddlers' Willingness to Taste Fruit and Vegetables." *Appetite* 53, 450–453 10.1016/j.appet.2009.08.012.

Heath, P., Houston-Price, C., & Kennedy, O. B. 2014. "Let's Look at Leeks! Picture Books Increase Toddlers' Willingness to Look at, Taste, and Consume Unfamiliar Vegetables." *Frontiers in Psychology, 5*, Article 191. https://doi.org/10.3389/fpsyg.2014.00191.

Jenkinson, C.E., Dickens, A.P., Jones, K. *et al.* 2013. "Is Volunteering a Public Health Intervention? A Systematic Review and Meta-analysis of the Health and Survival of Volunteers." *BMC Public Health* 13, 773. https://doi.org/10.1186/1471-2458-13-773.

Katz, D. 2011. Interview with David Katz, "The Truth about Food." *Bluezones..* https://www.bluezones.com/2018/11/author-of-truth-about-food-reveals-3-truths-to-end-all-confusion-about-a-healthy-diet/.

Milkie, M.A., Nomaguchi, K.M. and Denny, K.E. 2015. "Does the Amount of Time Mothers Spend With Children or Adolescents Matter?" *Journal of Marriage and Family*, 77: 355-372. https://doi.org/10.1111/jomf.12170.

LeBourgeois M. K., Hale L., Chang A. M., Akacem L. D., Montgomery-Downs H. E., Buxton O. M. 2017. "Digital Media and Sleep in Childhood and Adolescence." *Pediatrics*. 2017 Nov;140(Suppl 2):S92-S96. doi: 10.1542/peds.2016-1758J. PMID: 29093040; PMCID: PMC5658795.

Poti, Jennifer M. Michelle A. Mendez, Shu Wen Ng, Barry M. Popkin. 2015. "Is the Degree of Food Processing and Convenience Linked with the Nutritional Quality of Foods Purchased by US Households?" *The American Journal of Clinical Nutrition*, Volume 101, Issue 6, June 2015, 1251–1262, https://doi.org/10.3945/ajcn.114.100925.

Rogers, N. T., Demakakos, P., Taylor, M. S., Steptoe, A., Hamer, M., & Shankar, A. 2016. "Volunteering Is Associated with Increased Survival in Able-Bodied Participants of the English Longitudinal Study of Ageing. *Journal of Epidemiology and Community Health*, 70(6), 583–588. https://doi.org/10.1136/jech-2015-206305,

Spector, N. 2017. "Smiling can trick your brain into happiness—and boost your health." NBC Better by Today, November 28, 2017. https://www.nbcnews.com/better/health/ -your-brain-happiness-boost-your-health -ncna822591.

Wahlstrom, K., Dretzke, B., Gordon, M., Peterson, K., Edwards, K., Gdula, J. 2014. "Examining the Impact of Later School Start Times on the Health and Academic Performance of High School Students: A Multisite Study." St Paul, MN: University of Minnesota, Center for Applied Research and Educational Improvement.

Wasinek, B. 2006. Nutritional Gatekeepers and the 72% Solution. *Journal of the American Dietetic Association*, 106, 1324–1327.

ACKNOWLEDGMENTS

Writing this book has been an amazing journey in itself. None of this would have been possible without my family, my mindfulness teachers, the American Indian community, my colleagues, my friends, and all the ancestors who came before me.

I'm eternally grateful to my husband, Luke, and my daughters, Isabella and Sophia, for journeying with me on the mindful families path over the last eighteen years. In the community, it was Luke who provided the space for me to try new things with Native families. He supported me in venturing beyond the culturally-tailored, evidence-based family strengthening programs we were working with and expand into something that came from a more Indigenous world view. His support and belief along with the community's willingness to come along on the mindful journey with me and my many teachers and mentors was the seed that led to this book.

I also have to acknowledge my colleague and friend, Dr. Betsy Davis, who spent tireless hours on the phone and over email consulting, dreaming, and working with me on this book. I am forever indebted to her for this and many things. I also want to thank my friend Steve Mullensky for reading and editing and supporting my process, Dr. Bonnie Duran for just being an amazing inspiration, Diana Winston for being a wonderful model of a mindful family, and Dr. Burt Bialik for introducing me to Thich Nhat Hanh. And thank you to my mom, dad, and my bigger circle of extended family.

Finally, I want to thank Parallax Press who believed in me. Jacob Surpin, thank you for noticing, and Hisae Matsuda, thank you for seeing the vision and giving me this chance.

ABOUT THE AUTHOR

Renda Dionne Madrigal, PhD, is a licensed clinical psychologist, registered drama therapist, President of Mindful Practice Inc., and member of the Turtle Mountain Band of Chippewa Indians. She is also a mentor for the UCLA Mindfulness Awareness Teacher Training Program and is on the faculty at the Drama Therapy Institute of Los Angeles and California Indian Nations College. Featured on the cover of *Mindful* magazine in 2018, her workshops on mindful families, story medicine, and therapeutic theatre are popular nationally in the United States. In her clinical practice, Madrigal offers Mindfulness-Based Therapy, Somatic Experiencing, and narrative and drama (Narradrama) therapy for both adults and children. She has more than twenty years of experience creating and directing culturally tailored, evidence-based family and child programs for better health. She regularly incorporates storytelling, writing, and mindfulness into her work. She loves writing stories with Indigenous female protagonists working to save the world, and acts in Indigenous plays (healing ceremonies) with her family, written by her two Cahuilla-Chippewa daughters: *Menil and Her Heart* and *Wildflower: The Soul of an Indian.* She lives in Temecula, California.

Monastics and visitors practice the art of mindful living in the tradition of Thich Nhat Hanh at our mindfulness practice centers around the world. To reach any of these communities, or for information about how individuals, couples, and families can join in a retreat, please contact:

Plum Village
33580 Dieulivol, France
plumvillage.org

La Maison de l'Inspir
77510 Villeneuve-sur-Bellot, France
maisondelinspir.org

Magnolia Grove Monastery
Batesville, MS 38606, USA
magnoliagrovemonastery.org

Healing Spring Monastery
77510 Verdelot, France
healingspringmonastery.org

Blue Cliff Monastery
Pine Bush, NY 12566, USA
bluecliffmonastery.org

Stream Entering Monastery
Beaufort, Victoria 3373, Australia
nhapluu.org

Deer Park Monastery
Escondido, CA 92026, USA
deerparkmonastery.org

Thailand Plum Village
Nakhon Ratchasima
30130 Thailand
thaiplumvillage.org

European Institute
of Applied Buddhism
D-51545 Waldbröl, Germany
eiab.eu

Asian Institute of Applied Buddhism
Ngong Ping, Lantau Island,
Hong Kong
pvfhk.org

The Mindfulness Bell, a journal of the art of mindful living in the tradition of Thich Nhat Hanh, is published three times a year by our community. To subscribe or to see the worldwide directory of Sanghas, or local mindfulness groups, visit mindfulnessbell.org.

THICH NHAT HANH FOUNDATION

planting seeds of Compassion

The Thich Nhat Hanh Foundation works to continue the mindful
teachings and practice of Zen Master Thich Nhat Hanh, in order
to foster peace and transform suffering in all people, animals,
plants, and our planet. Through donations to the Foundation,
thousands of generous supporters ensure the continuation of Plum
Village practice centers and monastics around the world, bring
transformative practices to those who otherwise would not be able
to access them, support local mindfulness initiatives, and bring
humanitarian relief to communities in crisis in Vietnam.

By becoming a supporter, you join many others who want
to learn and share these life-changing practices of mindfulness,
loving speech, deep listening, and compassion for oneself,
each other, and the planet.

For more information on how you can help support
mindfulness around the world, or to subscribe to the
Foundation's monthly newsletter with teachings, news,
and global retreats, **visit tnhf.org**.

**PARALLAX
PRESS**

Parallax Press, a nonprofit publisher founded by
Zen Master Thich Nhat Hanh, publishes books and media
on the art of mindful living and Engaged Buddhism.
We are committed to offering teachings that help
transform suffering and injustice. Our aspiration is to
contribute to collective insight and awakening, bringing
about a more joyful, healthy, and compassionate society.

View our entire library at
parallax.org